Valuation

Valuation

Methods and Models in Applied Corporate Finance

George Chacko

Carolyn L. Evans

Associate Publisher: Amy Neidlinger
Executive Editor: Jeanne Glasser Levine
Operations Specialist: Jodi Kemper
Cover Designer: Chuti Prasertsith
Managing Editor: Kristy Hart
Project Editor: Elaine Wiley
Copy Editor: Keith Cline
Proofreader: Chuck Hutchinson
Indexer: Erika Millen
Senior Compositor: Gloria Schurick
Manufacturing Buyer: Dan Uhrig

This book is sold with the understanding that neither the authors nor the publisher is engaged in rendering legal, accounting, or other professional services or advice by publishing this book. Each individual situation is unique. Thus, if legal or financial advice or other expert assistance is required in a specific situation, the services of a competent professional should be sought to ensure that the situation has been evaluated carefully and appropriately. The author and the publisher disclaim any liability, loss, or risk resulting directly or indirectly from the use or application of any of the contents of this book.

For information about buying this title in bulk quantities, or for special sales opportunities (which may include electronic versions; custom cover designs; and content particular to your business, training goals, marketing focus, or branding interests), please contact our corporate sales department at corpsales@pearsoned.com or (800) 382-3419.

For government sales inquiries, please contact governmentsales@pearsoned.com.

For questions about sales outside the U.S., please contact international@pearsoned.com.

Company and product names mentioned herein are the trademarks or registered trademarks of their respective owners.

Printed in the United States of America

First Printing April 2014

ISBN-10: 0-13-290522-1
ISBN-13: 978-0-13-290522-0

Pearson Education LTD.
Pearson Education Australia PTY, Limited.
Pearson Education Singapore, Pte. Ltd.
Pearson Education Asia, Ltd.
Pearson Education Canada, Ltd.
Pearson Educación de Mexico, S.A. de C.V.
Pearson Education—Japan
Pearson Education Malaysia, Pte. Ltd.

Library of Congress Control Number: 2014930801

This book is dedicated to Leah and Shreya.
The world is a wondrous place.
We hope that you go out and
find it as intellectually stimulating
to explore as we have.

Contents

About the Authors

George Chacko is Associate Professor of Finance at Santa Clara University's Leavey School of Business and Founding Partner of HNC Advisors AG. He was formerly Associate Professor at Harvard Business School, Managing Director at State Street Bank, and Chief Investment Officer at Auda Alternative Investments. He holds a Ph.D. and M.A. in Business Economics from Harvard University and a B.S. from MIT.

Carolyn L. Evans is Senior Assistant Dean at the Leavey School of Business at Santa Clara University. She has worked at Intel Corporation, the Federal Reserve Bank of New York, the Federal Reserve Board of Governors, and the White House Council of Economic Advisers. She holds a Ph.D. and M.A. in Economics and a B.A. in East Asian Languages and Civilizations, all from Harvard University.

Preface

The past 40 years have seen a substantial change in how corporate financial managers (CFOs, treasurers, comptrollers) make investment decisions. Where the rule used to be to simply earn enough money on an investment, with enough being defined by various rules of thumb, one's intuition, or as simply any amount greater than the investment itself. Today, corporate financial managers use substantially more sophisticated frameworks to determine whether an investment is worthwhile or to determine at what price an investment is worthwhile. These frameworks entail the integration of basic finance principles with accounting, asset pricing models, and probabilistic and statistical techniques. One of the most powerful enabling factors for this trend is the increase in the availability of data and computational tools. Although valuation frameworks have existed for several decades, the lack of data, and to some extent, the lack of computational tools, made the application of these frameworks all but impossible. That has changed considerably today. In fact, the application of valuation frameworks has gone beyond the simple corporate budgeting context and has extended to mergers and acquisitions (M&A); private equity transactions, such as leveraged buyouts (LBOs); investment banking; and commercial real estate and infrastructure transactions. As a result, anyone working in corporate treasury, strategic planning, underwriting, M&A, private equity, or strategic consulting needs to understand the valuation techniques of modern corporate finance.

This book is intended for a reader who has some understanding of basic financial management, such as the role and application of discounted cash flows (DCF). We start from the DCF framework and build up to the valuation models that are widely used in practice. Instead of simply telling you what is done, this book focuses on explaining to you why the frameworks used in practice are valid and why certain shortcuts are taken.

This is not a general corporate finance book. Corporate finance is a huge field, and even those books that try to just give an overview of the whole field tend to be hundreds of pages long. Instead, this book focuses specifically on valuation. We cover as much about corporate finance as needed to develop the valuation techniques widely used in practice. However, we try to keep this book tight and focused, and therefore rarely stray into the field of corporate finance beyond valuation.

Readers are expected to have some basic mathematical knowledge of algebra, probability, and statistics. Nothing beyond this level of mathematics is assumed in the book. Where certain mathematical techniques are needed, we develop and explain these as we go along.

We hope that you find this a valuable starting point for learning about the broad and extremely rich field of corporate finance. Both academics and practitioners have published a great deal of literature published about corporate finance. The research in this field ongoing, and as a result, the knowledge base in this field continues to grow every day.

1

Introduction

1.1 Introduction

Every day, businesses face decision choices. For example, should a bank choose to expand organically by opening new branches, or should it expand by acquiring another bank with its own network of branches. Or, should a technology company release a new version of a product line now, and thereby cannibalize sales of its existing product line, or should it wait a year at the risk of giving its competitors time to catch up. The key to success in business is to make sound, or value-creating, business decisions. Every choice a business manager can potentially make has risk associated with it.[1] In turn, every choice also has some upside, or positive return, associated with it. A sound decision is one that balances this risk and return to create value for the owners of the business, whether those are public shareholders or a private ownership group.[2] However, to make value-creating business decisions, a manager needs to be able to first quantify, or measure, the risk and return inherent in each of the decision choices he is facing, and then convert these risk-return combinations into ex-ante measures of value creation. This is where the topic of valuation comes into play. Valuation is simply the conversion of risk and return into monetary value. The value could be of intangible assets like ideas or potential projects, or it could be of tangible assets like a manufacturing plant or the shares of a business. The common theme underlying valuation, however, is that it allows managers to make better business decisions by quantifying into a single metric the risk and return inherent in all business decision choices.

Every decision that a business faces can be conceptualized as a node on a decision tree, as shown in Figure 1.1. A manager facing a decision is trying to decide which of multiple paths emanating from this node he wants to take for the business. The figure illustrates the example of a manager deciding whether to build a manufacturing plant. The two possible paths are to build the plant or to not build the plant. Once the initial decision to build or not build is made, the decision tree branches off again into the capacity of the plant and again to the number of assembly lines. Each of the branches represents a set of possible outcomes that could occur. The role of valuation, then, is to quantify the value created (or destroyed) by deciding to head down a specific path. For example, the value created by building a plant with a 100,000 unit capacity containing one large assembly line would need to be quantified, as would the value created by not building a plant at all.

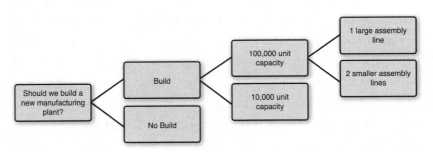

Figure 1.1 Decision tree for building a manufacturing plant

Note, however, that this path is only a decision path; it is not an outcome path. While a manager may decide to take a particular path, the result from taking the path is uncertain, and it might take many years before it becomes a known quantity. A more quantitative way to state this is that there is a probability distribution of possible results from the decision to take a path. Therefore, the process of valuation must take into account this probability distribution of outcomes (or risk) involved in taking a specific path.

1.2 Present Value

The standard measure that delivers the expected value created by a business decision, incorporating the full probability distribution of possible results, or payoffs, is present value. The present value of a business decision is defined mathematically as follows:

$$Value_0 = \frac{E(CF_1)}{1+r} + \frac{E(CF_2)}{(1+r)^2} + \frac{E(CF_3)}{(1+r)^3} + \dots \tag{1}$$

The result of evaluating the right-hand side of this equation is the value (at time 0) created by pursuing a business decision (for example, going down a specific node on the decision tree in Figure 1.1). On the right-hand side of Equation 1, $E(CF_1)$, $E(CF_2)$, and $E(CF_3)$ all denote expected cash flows in subsequent periods 1, 2, and 3 (the periods could be in months, quarters, years, and so on) due to undertaking the business decision, or project.[3] Note that these are expected future cash flows. The value creation measure is evaluated at time 0, at the very start of the project. Therefore, we are evaluating what would be the value created if this project is undertaken. Because we are calculating the value of pursuing this business decision at time period 0, before the uncertainty of the project has resolved itself, we have to put in our expectations of future cash flows rather than actual, or realized, cash flows.

In the denominator of Equation 1 is the discount rate, r. The discount rate denotes the expected return that a business expects for taking on the risk associated with the project.

Equation 1 is modeling the riskiness of the project under consideration as a set of risky cash flows. These cash flows are modeled as a set of probability distributions (see Figure 1.2). The mean of each distribution is captured by the expected value of each cash flow. In Figure 1.2, the first bell-shaped curve, with a mean of $E(CF_1)$, represents the probability distribution of the cash flows in period 1, the second curve (with a mean of $E(CF_2)$) represents the distribution of cash flows in period 2, and so on.

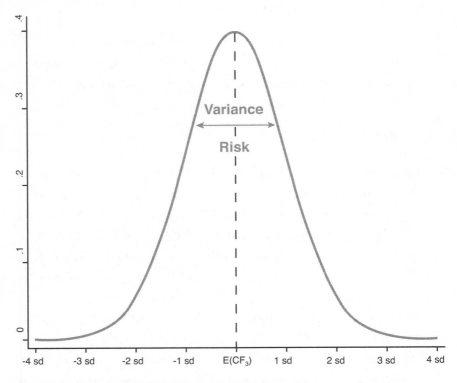

Figure 1.2 Probability distributions modeling a set of risky cash flows

The variance of each distribution gives us the risk of the cash flows. In Figure 1.2, the variance is given by the "width" of the bell-shaped curve. The wider the curve, the greater the range of possible cash flows generated by the project for that period. The area under the curve shows the likelihood of a given range of cash flow outcomes. For example, the area under the first curve and between the points minus one standard deviation (–1 sd) and plus one standard deviation (1 sd) gives the likelihood that the cash flow from the project in the first period will fall within one standard deviation of the mean expected cash flow. In Equation 1, the variance, or risk, of cash flows is captured by the discount rate. The higher the risk, the higher the discount rate; that is, the more risk that a business decision entails, the higher the expected return the business expects as compensation for taking that risk (if it decides to do so).

The number of terms on the right-hand side of Equation 1 depends on the number of periods over which the business will be earning cash flows for undertaking this project. All future time periods in which the business realizes cash flows from undertaking this project, no matter how far out into the future these might be, need to be incorporated.

Although it might seem simplistic initially, this present value equation is the foundation for all of modern finance and, in particular, the topic of our book: financial valuation. Of course, the formula itself is easy to understand, but implementing it in practical business settings is the real challenge. In many ways, to do this well is an art. The goal of this book is to introduce the basics and a few advanced concepts about how to apply valuation to practical business problems that executives face.

1.3 Financial Statements and Analysis

The first step for implementing valuation is to understand exactly what we are trying to value. From a conceptual standpoint, it helps to have a couple of diagrams in mind when doing any type of valuation activity: the financial statements for the project. Figure 1.3 shows a balance sheet for a possible project that a firm is considering undertaking. For the purpose of valuation, all economic agents/quantities, whether they are companies, people, or assets (tangible or intangible), can be represented by balance sheets and income statements. We use this concept throughout this book. So, if you are unsure how to do this or find it hard to think about this conceptually, the book will provide many examples. Figure 1.3 is our first example of this. It denotes the balance sheet representation (as well as its associated income statement representation) of a project (in this case, the construction of a manufacturing plant). As with any balance sheet, the left-hand side represents the assets (in this case, the manufacturing plant), and the right-hand side represents the liabilities and the owners', or shareholders', equity.[4] When we are doing a valuation, we are always valuing some part of this balance sheet. The income statement is a representation of the various cash flows produced by (or operating) the asset on the left-hand side of the balance sheet.

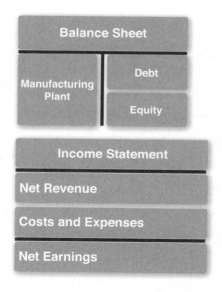

Figure 1.3 ABC Company project balance sheet and income statement

Before we do a valuation, we want to make sure that we analyze all aspects of this balance sheet and its associated income statement. This is precisely the goal of Chapter 2, "Financial Statement Analysis." Chapter 2 discusses a few of the concepts and techniques to analyze this balance sheet and income statement. We will go through important linkages within the balance sheet, within the income statement, and across these two financial statements. We will also demonstrate some techniques to tease out what are the sensitive factors for success in these financial statements and how to figure these out. The goal of Chapter 2 is not to teach accounting; instead, we want to build on your existing foundation of knowledge in accounting to emphasize certain concepts and to introduce some new concepts that will prove particularly useful for valuation.

1.4 Financial Forecasting

The balance sheet and income statement in Figure 1.3 presents a static image of the project, as it looks at one point in time and the cash flows it produced in the time period just preceding that point in time. To conduct a valuation of a project, however, we need to figure out how a project will do over time, through the life of the project. Specifically, we need to figure out future payoffs, or cash flows, from the project if we are to use Equation 1. To do this, we need to figure out what the future balance sheets and income statements for this project will look like. So, we will have to learn how to forecast balance sheets and income statements. This is the goal of Chapter 3, "Financial Forecasting." Chapter 3 discusses simple, but commonly used, tools and techniques for forecasting income statement and balance sheets (and, indirectly, cash flow statements). A critical element of forecasting a balance sheet is to make sure that all the expected future balance sheets balance (that is, that the asset side equals the sum of liabilities and owners' equity). As you will discover, enforcing this constraint will give you the first critical input for Equation 1, expected future cash flows.

1.5 Free Cash Flows

After we have constructed pro forma, or projected, financial statements for the project that we are trying to value, we can calculate the expected future cash flows, $E(CF_1)$, $E(CF_2)$, ... needed for Equation 1. To illustrate this point, Figure 1.4 presents a projected balance sheet. The cash flows that need to be input into Equation 1 are known as *free cash flows* and are depicted in Figure 1.4 by the arrow labeled Free Cash Flow. This diagram is conveying a picture of what precisely we are determining when we calculate free cash flows for a present value computation. For a typical project at a typical company, the left-hand side of the balance sheet represents the "business," while the right-hand side represents the financing. Therefore, the left-hand side of the balance sheet generates the revenues and nonfinancing costs associated with the project.[5] These cash flows flow from the left-hand side to the right-hand side. The right-hand side can be broken down crudely into debt and equity. Therefore, the cash flows that are being generated by the business are flowing to those entities that are financing the business: the debt holders and the equity holders. If we want to do a valuation from the perspective of all financial claimants (both debt and equity holders), the cash flows used in Equation 1 are the free cash flows. This would produce a value for the entire left-hand side of the balance sheet. Chapter 4, "Free Cash Flows," covers this concept of free cash flows and goes into the detail about how to calculate free cash flows. The goal of Chapter 4 is to be able to produce all the numbers needed for the numerators in Equation 1 for any business project or company that one might want to value.

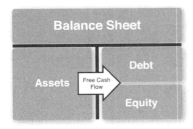

Figure 1.4 ABC Company projected balance sheet

1.6 Discount Rates

Once the numerators in Equation 1 are calculated, all that is needed to do a valuation is to calculate the denominators in Equation 1. This is the goal of Chapter 5, "Cost of Capital." Calculating this cost of capital (or equivalently, the required/expected rate of return)[6] for a project is actually a difficult task, and one that the field of finance is still heavily researching. As a result, there is no universally agreed-upon methodology for doing these calculations.[7] Chapter 5 presents a couple of the basic theories for determining the cost of capital and then also shows a couple of methods that are used in practice. Regardless of how one chooses to calculate a cost of capital, the procedure for decomposition of this value into other cost of capital values, such as cost of debt capital and cost of equity capital, is universally agreed upon, and this is what we cover next in Chapter 5. Included in this discussion is a measure called the *asset cost of capital*.

The discussion of these topics naturally brings up the question of how capital structure affects the expected return of the left-hand side of the balance sheet. It is at this point that we will discuss the implications of financing choices such as tax shields and costs of financial distress. As shown in Figure 1.5, these financing implications alter the value of the left-hand side of the balance sheet (and consequently the right-hand side as well), which in turn affects cost of capital calculations. Therefore, an important part of the discussion in Chapter 5 is the procedure for calculating the cost of capital taking into account the effects of capital structure decisions.

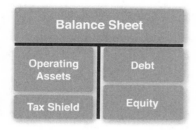

Figure 1.5 Implications of financing choices

1.7 Valuation Frameworks

Chapter 6, "Putting It All Together: Valuation Frameworks," pulls all the concepts presented in the previous chapters together and shows how to evaluate Equation 1 and determine a measure of value for a project. At the end of Chapter 5, we explain how the creation of costs and benefits due to capital structure decisions, such as tax shields, alters the value of the left-hand side of the balance sheet. This means that the cash flow effects of capital structure decisions need to be projected out so that the present value implications of these decisions can be measured. This leads to two different ways of computing the present value of a project using Equation 1, depending on how changes in the capital structure are likely to occur. We will first demonstrate the technique known as *adjusted present value* (APV). APV incorporates the effects of all time-varying capital structure decisions and is therefore a universal methodology for evaluating the present value of a project. However, in the special case where the debt-to-equity ratio of a project is kept constant through time, we will show that the APV approach can be simplified to another approach utilizing the *weighted average cost of capital* (WACC).[8] The WACC-based approach allows for a much simpler and faster evaluation of Equation 1, but it can be used only under the restriction that the proportion of debt and equity on the right-hand side of the balance sheet remain the same through time (though the total amount of debt and equity may increase or decrease through time). Finally, we will introduce another special case of APV in Chapter 6 known as *flow to equity* (FTE). The FTE approach is widely used in the field of private equity, especially in buyout situations. We will show how to utilize FTE and how FTE evolves from APV, and we will also show FTE's relationship to WACC.

1.8 Summary

In summary, we have organized the book according to the sequence one would generally follow in performing a valuation. Chapter 2 shows how to perform preliminary financial analysis on a potential business project. Our goal ultimately is to be able to evaluate the present value relation in Equation 1 for the project at hand. Chapter 3 starts this process by demonstrating how to calculate future financial statements for the project. Chapter 4 then shows how you take these forecasts and generate free cash flow forecasts, the numerator in Equation 1. Chapter 5 then presents several approaches for calculating a discount rate, the denominator in Equation 1, for the project. In Chapter 5, you also learn that financing choices can have value implications for any project. Chapter 6 shows how to incorporate these value implications in the evaluation of Equation 1. In Chapter 6, we also bring together the evaluation of the numerator and denominator of Equation 1 to finish the valuation. Thus, by the end of this book, you should have a solid conceptual understanding of valuation as well as a substantial amount of practical knowledge about how to go about executing a valuation of a potential business decision.

Endnotes

1 Even not making a choice has a risk (an opportunity risk of sorts).

2 This concept also applies to nonprofits, where the endowment of the nonprofit may be thought of as the shareholder that potentially accrues value.

3 It is important to distinguish subsequent periods of time versus subsequent decisions on a one-period decision tree (such as in Figure 1.1). Equation 1 contains cash flows over multiple time periods for a single decision path (with multiple decision nodes, such as in Figure 1.1) that was chosen at time 0.

4 The right side is also commonly thought of as the financing structure of the left-hand side. Therefore, in Figure 1.3, the right-hand side is composed of a set of investors who provided debt financing for the manufacturing plant and a set of investors who provided equity financing. Another common view of the right-hand side is as the ownership structure. The equity holders own the asset(s) on the left-hand side, but if equity holders cannot pay the debt holders what they are due, the debt holders will take ownership of the asset(s).

5 It is important to note here that this statement does not hold true if the project is a financial institution. For financial institutions, the "business" is on both the left- and right-hand sides of the balance sheet. For example, the business of a bank might be to take deposits and make loans. However, the deposits would be on the right-hand side of the balance sheet, while the loans are on the left-hand side. We discuss this in more detail later in the book.

6 We use the terms *cost of capital, required rate of return, expected rate of return,* and *discount rate* interchangeably throughout the book. All of these terms refer to the discount rate used to discount cash flows.

7 This is one of the reasons that we see a proliferation of investment funds in the world. If two fund managers cannot agree on the expected rate of return on, for example, a business, one may decide to buy shares in that business, while one decides to sell shares in the same business.

8 Because this approach uses WACC, it is often referred to simply as the *WACC approach*.

2

Financial Statement Analysis

2.1 Introduction

Before you value a project, such as a firm, you must conduct some basic financial due diligence to assess the financial position of the firm. The financial position of a firm determines its success or failure. If its debt gets too high, its cash balances fall too low, its operating margins are too low, and so on, it will not likely survive much longer. Financial health provides the firm with more flexibility in dealing with unexpected developments. All firms use a fairly standard way of reporting on their financial positions. Understanding these standard ways in which firms report is a powerful tool for analyzing the performance of an organization. Three particular statements—income statements, balance sheets, and cash flow statements—are the key to understanding financial reporting. Although separate statements, these three are intricately linked to each other, as discussed throughout this chapter.

2.2 Financial Statement Analysis

Balance sheets, income statements, and cash flow statements together provide a summary of a firm's financial position. Each provides a separate set of information, but they are all also linked to each other and jointly determined. Figures 2.1 and 2.2 illustrate how the linkages work. Very broadly speaking, the balance sheet is a static statement (a "snapshot") of a firm's position at a given point in time, usually the end of a quarter or a year. The cash flow and income statements record the way in which a firm moves from the balance sheet at the end of one period to the balance sheet at the end of the next period. In other words, the cash flow statement and income statement provide "links"[1] between one period of time and the next.

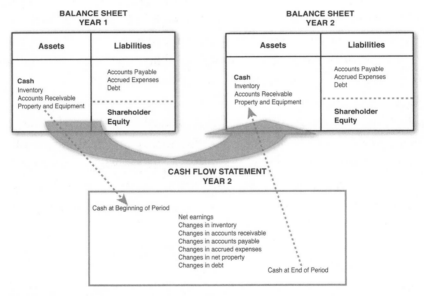

Figure 2.1 Relationship between balance sheet and cash flow statement

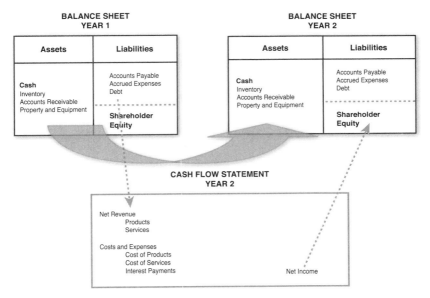

Figure 2.2 Relationship between balance sheet and income statement

For example, as Figure 2.1 shows, cash at the end of the year shows up on the asset side of the balance sheet in Year 1, and also as Cash at Beginning of Period in the cash flow statement for Year 2. Within the cash flow statement, as explained in more detail later in this chapter, activities that generated or used cash during Year 2 are recorded. What's left at the end of the year (Cash at End of Period) shows up as Cash in the balance sheet for Year 2. As another example, the change from accounts receivable at the end of Year 1 and accounts receivable at the end of Year 2 will result in cash being generated or used. This amount will then show up in the cash flow statement for the end of Year 2. Similarly, as shown in Figure 2.2, the income statement provides a link between the balance sheets for two consecutive periods. For example, part of the change between inventory at the end of Year 1 and inventory at the end of Year 2 will show up as revenue in the income statement as well as cost of products (sometimes referred to as *cost of goods sold*, or COGS) in the income statement. Net income generated during the year (shown in the lower-right side of the income statement in Figure 2.2) flows into shareholder equity in Year 2's balance sheet. In this chapter, we provide more details on each of these financial statements, as well as on the linkages among them.

2.2.1 Balance Sheets

Balance sheets provide a snapshot of a firm's financial position at a point in time. They record the assets and liabilities of a firm at a specified time. Figure 2.3 provides the balance sheet for ABC Company for 2011, 2012, and 2013. Balance sheets are divided into three major categories. Assets entries represent property, intangible assets, and other items that a firm owns and that have value. Within assets, individual entries may be either "current assets" or other assets. Current assets are those that are relevant to the near term (that is, the period of the financial statement, in the sense that they could be converted into cash fairly quickly). For ABC Company, these current assets include cash ($670 million), accounts receivable ($1.52 billion), and inventory ($624 million) at the end of 2013. ABC's total current assets are $4.25 billion at the end of 2013. (Figure 2.3a provides definitions of the individual items in the balance sheet.)

Figure 2.3 ABC Co. Balance Sheet

ASSETS	Oct-13	Oct-12	Oct-11
Current assets:			
Cash and cash equivalents	670	911	1,107
Accounts receivable	1,519	1,540	1,378
Financing receivables	264	249	223
Inventory	624	539	511
Other current assets	1,175	1,277	1,160
Total current assets	4,252	4,515	4,378
Property, plant and equipment	1,024	980	939
Long-term financing receivables and other assets	896	1,019	941
Other Long Term Assets	6,975	5,477	4,197
Total assets	13,147	11,992	10,455
LIABILITIES AND STOCKHOLDERS' EQUITY			
Current liabilities:			
Notes payable and short-term borrowings	674	587	154
Accounts payable	1,229	1,197	1,234
Employee compensation and benefits	333	355	339
Taxes on earnings	87	67	76
Deferred revenue	621	561	515
Accrued restructuring	55	76	92
Other accrued liabilities	1,205	1,275	1,173
Total current liabilities	4,204	4,117	3,584
Long-term debt	1,879	1,272	1,165
Other liabilities	1,460	1,588	1,421
Total liabilities	7,543	6,977	6,170
Stockholders' equity:			
ABC stockholders' equity			
Preferred stock, $0.01 par value			
Common stock, $0.01 par value	2	2	2
Additional paid-in capital	1,150	1,150	1,150
Retained earnings	4,453	3,863	3,133
Total ABC stockholders' equity	5,604	5,015	4,285
Total stockholders' equity	5,604	5,015	4,285
Total liabilities and stockholders' equity	13,147	11,992	10,455

Note: All figures are in millions of dollars.

Figure 2.3a Balance Sheet Terms

Term	Definition
Current assets	Assets that could be converted into cash or used within the next year.
Cash	Cash and related financial assets. The most liquid of assets.
Accounts receivable	Payments due within the next year from goods or services sold.
Inventory	Materials, supplies, and finished goods on hand. Intended to be sold to customers.
Other current assets	Other assets to be converted to cash or used within the next year.
Property, plant, and equipment	Real estate, buildings, machinery, and other long-lived physical assets.
Long-term financing receivables	Payments due in more than one year on loans, leases, etc. provided to others.
Goodwill	Excess over book value of acquired assets. An intangible asset.
Purchased intangible assets	Assets that have no physical presence, such as an intellectual property right.
Current liabilities	Payments owed within the next year.
Notes payable and short-term borrowings	Payments due on borrowings within the next year.
Accounts payable	Payments due to suppliers within the next year.
Employee compensation and benefits	Salaries and benefits to employees.
Taxes on earnings	Taxes due on earnings.
Deferred revenue	Revenue received for which a good or service has not been fully provided.
Long-term debt	Payments due on borrowings beyond one year.
Total stockholders' equity	Total capital value. Net worth.

Sources: Authors and Financial Accounting Standards Board

Noncurrent assets are those that are less readily transferable into cash or have a longer life. Examples for ABC include property, plant, and equipment ($1.02 billion at the end of 2013) and long-term financing receivables ($896 million). Clearly, converting a physical plant into cash takes longer than, for example, converting inventory into cash; this distinction between the two is the reason why inventory is placed under current assets and why property, plants, and equipment are placed within other assets. The distinction between current and other assets is important because it gives some idea of a firm's access to cash within a relatively short time horizon. As discussed later in this chapter, the value of current assets is also critical in thinking about a firm's ability to cover its short-term liabilities. Adding together ABC's current and noncurrent assets, its total assets for 2013 are $13.1 billion.

The second major category of the balance sheet—liabilities—lists amounts that a firm owes to others. As with assets, liabilities are often divided into current liabilities and other liabilities. ABC's current liabilities include notes payable ($674 million at the end of 2013), accounts payable ($1.23 billion), and employee compensation ($333 million). Current liabilities represent an obligation to pay in the relative near term. In contrast, noncurrent liabilities include longer-term obligations, such as long-term debt ($1.88 billion at the end of 2013). For ABC, total liabilities, both current and noncurrent, in 2013 were $7.5 billion.

Shareholders' equity represents the third major category on the balance sheet. Shareholders' equity essentially measures the net worth of a firm. It is the cumulative result of profits produced by the firm plus any inflows and outflows of cash to shareholders. It is an important indicator of a firm's financial health and, as discussed later, provides a buffer against negative results in the business. Another term for shareholder equity is *equity capital*.[2]

These three categories—assets, liabilities, and shareholders' equity—are linked to each other, in the following way:

Assets = Liabilities + Shareholders' Equity   (1)

This relationship must always hold and provides important information about the linkages among all of a firm's activities. If any asset category increases in value, either liabilities or shareholder equity must also go up. In other words, balance sheets must *always* balance. Turning again to ABC's 2013 results, we see that Total Assets = $13.1 billion = $7.5 billion + $5.6 billion = Total Liabilities + Total Stockholders' Equity.

2.2.2 Income Statements

In contrast to the snapshot nature of the balance sheet, the income statement shows changes during the reporting period. The income statement records the flows in and out of income over the course of a year. Figure 2.4 shows ABC's income statement for the years 2011, 2012, and 2013. (Figure 2.4a provides definitions of the entries in the income statement.)

Figure 2.4 ABC Co. Income Statement

	Oct-13	Oct-12	Oct-11
Net revenue:			
Products	7,063	7,067	6,171
Services	3,503	3,401	3,344
Financing income	37	35	31
Total net revenue	10,604	10,503	9,546
Costs and expenses:			
Cost of products	5,431	5,422	4,709
Cost of services	2,671	2,549	2,555
Financing interest	26	25	27
Research and development	271	247	235
Selling, general and administrative	1,122	1,060	971
Amortization of purchased intangible assets	134	124	132
Impairment of goodwill and purchased intangible assets	74		
Restructuring charges	54	95	53
Acquisition-related charges	15	24	20
Total operating expenses	9,797	9,546	8,701
Earnings from operations	806	957	845
Interest and other, net	(58)	(42)	(60)

	Oct-13	Oct-12	Oct-11
Earnings before taxes	749	915	785
Provision for taxes	159	184	146
Net earnings	590	730	638
Net earnings per share:			
Basic	0.28	0.32	0.27
Diluted	0.28	0.31	0.26
Weighted-average shares used to compute net earnings per share:			
Basic	175	193	199
Diluted	177	198	203

Note: Entries in parentheses represent negative numbers. All figures are in millions of dollars.

Figure 2.4a Income Statement Terms

Term	Definition
Net revenue	Earnings from products and/or services sold during the reporting period.
Net revenue - Financing income	Income from loans made to others.
Cost of products	Costs to produce products.
Cost of services	Costs to produce services.
Financing interest	Payments made to finance a purchase or use.
	For example, the expense incurred when leasing equipment.
Research and development	Costs of R and D.
Selling, general, and administrative	General costs of doing business. Includes ...
Amortization of intangible assets	Similar to depreciation, but a gradual write-down of intangible assets.
Restructuring charges	Charges associated with restructuring, such as severance costs for employees and exit costs.
Interest and other, net	Net interest payments.
Net earnings	Net revenue minus costs and expenses minus interest minus taxes. Net profit.

Sources: Authors and Financial Accounting Standards Board.

In the broadest sense, the income statement is divided into two categories: activities generating positive income (net revenue in Figure 2.4) and activities that generate negative income (costs and expenses in Figure 2.4). Within these broad categories fall specific types of activities that either increase or reduce income. For example, in the case of ABC, in 2013 the firm generated $7.06 billion in product revenue and $3.50 billion in revenue from selling services. Activities that subtracted from revenue included the costs incurred in producing the goods sold ($5.43 billion) and research and development costs ($271 million). To calculate the total earnings from operations, you subtract the total operating expenses from the total net revenue. As shown in Figure 2.4, ABC had earnings from operations of $806 million in 2013. (Of course, if operating expenses are greater than total net revenue, earnings from operations will be negative.)

After listing income and expenses and calculating earnings for operations, two additional nonoperational categories are accounted for before calculating the final net earnings for the year. The costs from interest payments are subtracted out ($58 million for ABC). The cost of paying taxes must also be accounted for ($159 million). After netting out these last two categories, the end result is net income. In 2013, ABC's net earnings were around $590 million. In other words, the cumulative results of income generating activities and income losing activities for ABC in 2013 were about $590 million. Again, this number could be negative, in which case ABC would have had a net loss for the year.

You can also think about the income statement as keeping track of the ways in which a balance sheet changes from year to year. It records the operational factors that affect a firm's income, or profits, from year to year. The value of net income (that is, the net result of all activity recorded in the balance sheet) over the course of a year then feeds directly into shareholders' equity for that year. For example, net income for ABC for 2013, $590 million, is equal to the change in retained earnings between 2012 and 2013, as shown in the balance sheets for those two years, where the level changes from $3.86 billion to $4.45 billion.[3] Ultimately, an income statement may be used to reconcile shareholders' equity between one year and another.

2.3 Cash Flow Statement

As with the income statement, the cash flow statement records flows. It keeps track of flows of cash into and out of a company's accounts. In essence, it illustrates how a firm goes from its cash balances in one year to its cash balances in the next year. It records the ways in which a firm brings in cash and spends it.

Before discussing the cash flow statement itself, it is useful to introduce another important financial record: the *sources and uses of cash statement*. The sources and uses statement records the sources and uses of cash by a firm over the course of a year. These changes could fall within just about any area of the balance sheet. To put together the sources and uses statement, you must compare balance sheets between two points in time (for example, ABC's balance sheets for 2012 and 2013).

In Figure 2.5, we construct a sources and uses of cash statement for ABC for 2013. Figure 2.5 shows the 2012 and 2013 balance sheets, along with a column that represents the difference between the 2012 and 2013 numbers. The sign (with negative numbers in parentheses in Figure 2.5) in the column showing the difference indicates whether cash was used or generated. Thus, a negative entry represents cash used up by that account, and a positive entry represents cash generated by that account. The various entries illustrate the ways that cash is generated or spent by the firm.

Figure 2.5 ABC Co. Sources and Use of Cash

ASSETS	Oct-13	Oct-12	Sources/(Uses) of Cash°
Current assets:			
Cash and cash equivalents	670	911	241
Accounts receivable	1,519	1,540	21
Financing receivables	264	249	(15)
Inventory	624	539	(85)
Other current assets	1,175	1,277	102
Total current assets	4,252	4,515	
Property, plant and equipment	1,024	980	(44)
Long-term financing receivables and other assets	896	1,019	123
Other long term assets	6,975	5,477	(1,497)
Total assets	13,147	11,992	
LIABILITIES AND STOCK-HOLDERS' EQUITY			
Current liabilities:			
Notes payable and short-term borrowings	674	587	86
Accounts payable	1,229	1,197	32
Employee compensation and benefits	333	355	(21)
Taxes on earnings	87	67	21
Deferred revenue	621	561	60
Accrued restructuring	55	76	(21)
Other accrued liabilities	1,205	1,275	(70)
Total current liabilities	4,204	4,117	
Long-term debt	1,879	1,272	608
Other liabilities	1,460	1,588	(128)
Total liabilities	7,543	6,977	
Total Sources and Uses of Cash for the Year			**0**
Total Change in Cash for the Year			(241)
Stockholders' equity:			
ABC stockholders' equity			
Preferred stock, $0.01 par value (300 shares authorized; none issued)			

ASSETS	Oct-13	Oct-12	Sources/(Uses) of Cash°
Common stock, $0.01 par value (9,600 shares authorized; 1,991 and 2,204 shares issued and outstanding, respectively)	2	2	
Additional paid-in capital	1,150	1,150	
Retained earnings	4,453	3,863	
Total ABC stockholders' equity	5,604	5,015	
Total stockholders' equity	5,604	5,015	589
Total liabilities and stockholders' equity	13,147	11,992	

* Positive sign represents "source" of cash. Numbers in parentheses represent a negative sign and are "uses" of cash.

Note: All figures are in millions of dollars.

For example, a decrease in accounts receivable generates cash, because it means that outstanding money due from customers has fallen. For ABC, accounts receivable went from $1.54 billion in 2012 to $1.52 billion in 2013. This change implies an increase in (that is, a "source" of) cash in the amount of $21 million. An increase in inventories, in contrast, implies a use of cash, because money must be spent to boost inventory levels. For ABC, inventories changed from $539 million in 2012 to $624 million in 2013, implying a "use" of $85 million. As an example on the liabilities side of the balance sheet, notes payable changed from $587 million to $674 million, generating a source of cash of $86 million.[4]

To sum up, when all the sources and uses of cash during the year are added together, all the positive transactions (that is, sources) offset all the negative transactions (that is, uses), and all taken together sum to 0.[5] Finally, note that the change in cash for the year (–$241 million) is equal to the changes in cash in all the other (noncash) accounts when summed together. Therefore, ultimately, a cash flow statement is intended to show how to "bridge the gap" between a company's cash levels in one year to its cash levels in the next year. (Also see Figures 2.1 and 2.2.) To preview the next few paragraphs, this same

$241 million shows up in ABC's cash flow statement (see Figure 2.6) as the "(Decrease) increase in cash and cash equivalents." Therefore, the sources and uses of cash statement provides information complementary to the information in the cash flow statement.

Figure 2.6 ABC Co. Cash Flow Statement

	Oct-13	Oct-12	Oct-11
Cash flows from operating activities:			
Net earnings	590	730	638
Adjustments to reconcile net earnings to net cash provided by operating activities:			
Depreciation and amortization	415	402	398
Impairment of goodwill and purchased intangible assets	74		
Stock-based compensation expense	57	56	53
Provision for doubtful accounts and financing receivables	7	13	29
Provision for inventory	18	16	18
Restructuring charges	54	95	53
Deferred taxes on earnings	14	16	32
Excess tax benefit from stock-based compensation	(14)	(25)	(14)
Other, net	(4)	14	2
Changes in assets and liabilities:			
Accounts and financing receivables	(19)	(200)	(46)
Inventory	(104)	(23)	128
Accounts payable	23	(58)	(13)
Taxes on earnings	51	60	61
Restructuring	(84)	(111)	(103)
Other assets and liabilities	(24)	7	(122)
Net cash provided by operating activities	1,053	994	1,115
Cash flows from investing activities:			
Investment in property, plant and equipment	(378)	(344)	(308)
Proceeds from sale of property, plant and equipment	83	50	41
Purchases of available-for-sale securities and other investments	(8)	(4)	(13)

	Oct-13	Oct-12	Oct-11
Maturities and sales of available-for-sale securities and other investments	6	17	14
Payments in connection with business acquisitions, net of cash acquired	(873)	(675)	(33)
Proceeds from business divestiture, net	7	10	
Net cash used in investing activities	(1,163)	(947)	(298)
Cash flows from financing activities:			
(Payments) issuance of commercial paper and notes payable, net)	(106)	346	(571)
Issuance of debt	995	263	567
Payment of debt	(195)	(110)	(226)
Issuance of common stock under employee stock plans	75	218	153
Repurchase of common stock	(843)	(920)	(428)
Excess tax benefit from stock-based compensation	14	25	14
Cash dividends paid	(70)	(64)	(64)
Net cash used in financing activities	(131)	(243)	(556)
(Decrease) increase in cash and cash equivalents)	(241)	(196)	261
Cash and cash equivalents at beginning of period	911	1,107	846
Cash and cash equivalents at end of period	670	911	1,107

Note: Numbers in parentheses represent a negative sign. All figures are in millions of dollars.

Figure 2.6 provides ABC's cash flow statements for 2011, 2012, and 2013. Like the source and uses of cash statement, the cash flow statement also tracks the changes in cash from one year to the next. Indeed, the third line from the bottom of the table, "(Decrease) increase in cash and cash equivalents," is the exact same value that we showed in Figure 2.5: –$241 million. The cash flow statement differs from the sources and uses of cash statement in that the cash flow statement lists things not included in sources and uses and places all entries into three broad categories.

The format shown in Figure 2.6 (the cash flow statement) is useful because it quickly shows the ways in which cash is generated or used. We can see that cash flows arise from operating activities ($1.1 billion), investing activities (−$1.2 billion), and financing activities (−$131 million). These numbers show that, while ABC generated a lot of cash through its operating activities (that is, via selling its goods and services), its outflows of cash via its investing activities overwhelmed the positive operating balance. Looking more carefully at this account, we see that payments in connection with acquisitions represented the largest share of the negative balance for investing activities. Another "high-level" insight from ABC's 2013 cash flow statement is that financing activities also generated a slightly negative cash flow. This net result was generated by both issuance of debt (about $1 billion) and stock repurchases ($843 million).

With the overall importance of the cash flow statement and its main components in mind, we can turn to discussing some of the finer details of this report. The entire first third of the statement represents cash flows from operating activities and reports additions and subtractions needed to convert net earnings (as reported in the income statement) to a purely cash basis. This is necessary because the income statement itself includes things that are not associated with an inflow or outflow of cash, and these entries need to be adjusted for in net income.

For example, the cash flow statement includes an entry of $74 million of "Impairment of goodwill and purchased intangible assets." The income statement includes a cost for this same category in this same amount. Because impairment of goodwill and intangible assets, essentially the decline in value of intangible assets held by the firm, does not involve a cash flow (because the asset is intangible), it needs to be added back in to the cash flow statement, to counteract its recording as a cost in the income statement. This top third also includes entries that record changes in assets and liabilities that, although they do not show up in the income statement, generate or use cash. For example, as noted earlier, an increase in inventories implies a use of cash, because money must be spent for inventory purchases; this value thus must be subtracted from net earnings.

The second third of this table details the impact on cash balances of investing activities. As discussed earlier, payments in connection with acquisitions represented the largest share of the negative balance for investing activities. Investment in property, plant, and equipment was also a large negative value. The final third records the details on cash flows from financing activities. Here, activities that bring cash in are issuing debt and issuing stock. Uses of cash are paying debt, repurchasing stock, and paying dividends. (Later in this chapter, we discuss further the interpretation of the results in these different categories.)

The bottom third of the cash flow statement shows the cash impact of financing activities. Payments (issuance) of debt and commercial paper generate outflows (inflows) of cash. Similarly, when stock is issued, cash is generated, and when stock is repurchased, cash declines. Payouts of dividends also use cash.

The net change in cash over the course of the year is shown in the third line from the bottom of the cash flow statement, −$241 million. This number is the same as we noted in the sources and uses of cash statement. It is the difference between cash balances at the end of 2012 and cash balances at the end of 2013.

2.3.1 Generalizing the Flow Statement

Both income statements and cash flow statements record flows over the course of a reporting period. Both also focus on one particular entry on the balance sheet as the reconciling account. The cash flow statement reconciles to the cash account, and the income statement reconciles to shareholder equity. The key to both is recognizing that a flow must feed through to some part of the balance sheet. In essence, any other account on the balance sheet could be used as the reconciling account. Because cash and equity receive the most emphasis, the cash flow statement and income statement are the two most commonly used approaches.

2.4 Market Value Balance Sheets

In the previous section, we provided an overview of "accounting value" balance sheets. They are *accounting* value because all assets and liabilities are recorded at the value at which they were originally acquired. Another term for this value is *book value.* An alternative valuation format for a balance sheet is a *market value balance sheet.* It is exactly the same as an accounting value balance sheet, but assets and liabilities are recorded at their true market value. Just as with accounting value balance sheets, assets must equal liabilities plus shareholders' equity.

Market value balance sheets could look very different from accounting value balance sheets. For example, suppose that a piece of real estate was purchased 20 years ago and has since appreciated on a yearly basis. The market value balance sheet would record a much higher number than would the accounting value one. Similarly, suppose that a company builds a manufacturing plant that it depreciates on a straight-line basis over a 10-year period. At the end of 10 years, the plant would sit on the company's books under Property, Plant, & Equipment with zero value. However, the market value of the plant could easily be much higher than zero.

Market value balance sheets are one important distinguishing feature between accounting and finance. Finance is primarily concerned with the market values of assets, liabilities, and equity. Indeed, valuation is concerned with deriving the market value of something, usually on someone's or some firm's balance sheet. As we develop our valuation frameworks, we will be using the concept of market value balance sheets extensively. Many of the fundamental rules that apply for accounting balance sheets also apply for market value balance sheets.

For example, market value balance sheets must balance; and gains and losses in assets accrue (primarily) to shareholders' equity.

2.5 Financial Ratios

Accounting balance sheets, income statements, and cash flow statements provide a great deal of information on a firm's activities. To analyze the meaning and implications of this information, *financial ratios* are an important tool in financial statement analysis. In the most basic sense, most of these financial ratios are simply the ratio of one entry in a financial statement to another. However, when analyzed over time, especially in comparison to peer firms, or relative to an industry standard, they reveal a great deal about a firm's performance. This section explains some key financial ratios and uses ABC's financial statements to illustrate how to use them. Figure 2.7 provides a summary of the definitions of some key financial ratios.

Figure 2.7 Financial Ratios

Term	Definition
Return Ratios	
Return on Equity (ROE)	$\dfrac{\text{Net Earnings}}{\text{Stockholder's Equity}}$
Return on Assets (ROA)	$\dfrac{\text{Net Earnings}}{\text{Total Assets}}$
Asset Turnover	$\dfrac{\text{Net Revenue}}{\text{Total Assets}}$
Profit Margin	$\dfrac{\text{Net Earnings}}{\text{Net Revenue}}$
Borrowing Ratios	
Debt to Assets (Leverage)	$\dfrac{\text{Total Liabilities}}{\text{Total Assets}}$
Debt to Equity	$\dfrac{\text{Total Liabilities}}{\text{Stockholder's Equity}}$

Term	Definition
Assets to Equity (Leverage)	$\dfrac{\text{Total Assets}}{\text{Stockholder's Equity}}$
Interest Coverage	$\dfrac{\text{Net Income Before Taxes} + \text{Interest Expense}}{\text{Interest Expense}}$
Liquidity Ratios	
Current Ratio	$\dfrac{\text{Currents Assets}}{\text{Current Liabilities}}$
Quick Ratio	$\dfrac{\text{Current Assets} - \text{Inventory}}{\text{Current Liabilities}}$
Turnover	
Payables Period	$\dfrac{\text{Accounts Payable Purchases (or Total Cost of Goods Sold)}}{365}$
Inventory Days	$\dfrac{\text{Inventory Total Cost of Goods Sold}}{365}$
Collection Period	$\dfrac{\text{Accounts Receivable Total Net Revenue}}{365}$

Source: Authors.

2.5.1 Return Ratios

The first set of ratios shown in Figure 2.7 indicates the overall sales and earning performance of a firm. They show the revenue or earnings generated in relation to equity, assets, and revenue.

The *return on equity* (ROE) is the ratio of net earnings to total shareholders' equity. It shows the magnitude of earnings relative to the net worth of a firm. For ABC, this ratio is calculated by taking net earnings from the income statement ($590 million) and dividing by total shareholder equity from the balance sheet ($5.6 billion). This calculation yields an ROE of 11% for ABC in 2013.[6] As shareholders' equity is an indicator of shareholders' investment in the firm, the

ROE essentially indicates how much return a firm is able to produce for its shareholders' investments into the firm. It also indicates, for a given unit of stock, how effective a firm is at generating income.[7]

The *return on assets* (ROA) is the ratio of net earnings to total assets and indicates the magnitude of earnings relative to the total assets of a firm. To calculate this ratio for ABC, we again take 2013 net income from the income statement ($590 million), but this time divide by total assets at the end of 2013 ($13.1 billion), yielding a ratio of 4%. This ratio indicates, for a given unit of assets, how productive a firm is at generating income, in contrast to ROE, which provides the effectiveness relative to a unit of equity. Note that the ROA is necessarily lower than the ROE because assets are equal to the sum of shareholders' equity and liabilities. Also, a highly leveraged firm will have an ROE that is relatively much higher than the ROA in comparison to a firm that is less highly leveraged.

A third return ratio, *asset turnover* (also sometimes called asset *turns*), shows the value of net revenue (that is, total sales) relative to assets. As a firm is generating revenue, it is cycling through assets. For example, goods come into the firm and stay in inventory. When the firm generates revenue, it sells these goods, and they leave the inventory account. A similar process occurs for every account on the asset side of the balance sheet. Asset turnover indicates how many full cycles, or round trips, occur for total assets for a firm in one year due to revenue generation. For ABC, this calculation is total net revenue ($10.6 billion, as taken from the income statement) divided by total assets ($13.1 billion from the balance sheet), or 0.81. This indicates that the firm experiences 81% of a full asset cycle in one year, or that there is a full cycling through of assets in 1 / 0.81 = 1.23 years. In general, the more efficient a firm operates, the higher the asset turnover (and, consequently, the higher the ROA).[8]

Finally, the profit margin indicates how much of net revenue (total sales) feeds through into net earnings, and it is defined as net earnings divided by net revenue. A more profitable firm has a higher profit margin. For ABC, this ratio is net earnings of $590 million divided by net revenue of $10.6 billion, or .06. Note that a higher level of costs and expenses relative to revenue will necessarily drive a lower profit margin. The profit margin thus tells us something about how efficiently a firm is able to produce the revenue that it generates.

2.5.2 Leverage Ratios

Leverage, or borrowing, *ratios* indicate the degree of indebtedness (and, consequently, the level of financial risk) of a firm.

The *debt-to-assets ratio* (or *debt ratio*) shows the ratio of total liabilities to total assets. It provides an overall indication of a firm's indebtedness. For ABC, we need to divide total liabilities ($7.54 billion) in 2013 by total assets ($13.1 billion) to calculate a debt ratio of 57%. Recalling the identity introduced earlier

$$\text{Assets} = \text{Liabilities} + \text{Shareholders' Equity} \qquad (2)$$

we can see that a higher debt ratio also indicates a relatively higher level of liabilities to shareholders' equity, or debt-to-equity ratio. While a firm with a high debt ratio indicates more borrowing relative to assets, it may also indicate a firm that is able to generate a relatively high ROE, because the level of equity is relatively smaller in comparison to the level of debt.

The debt-to-equity ratio also provides an overall indication of indebtedness, as well as an indication of the composition of the right-hand side of the balance sheet, i.e., whether a firm is more heavily weighted towards debt or toward equity. For ABC, this number is $7.54 billion in debt divided by $5.60 billion in equity, or 1.3. The debt ratio is necessarily lower than the debt-to-equity ratio because assets = liabilities + shareholder equity.

Finally, the ratio of assets to equity provides another indicator of leverage.[9] Note that because assets − equity = liabilities, this ratio tells us about the leverage of the firm. A high ratio implies relatively high assets relative to equity, thus relatively high liabilities and thus leverage. A low ratio implies relatively low assets relative to equity, and thus relatively low liabilities and low leverage. For ABC, this ratio is 2.3.

Interest coverage provides a shorter-term perspective on the indebtedness maintained by the firm. It is a measure of the cash flow that a firm has available (calculated as net income before interest and taxes, or EBIT) to meet interest payments. This available cash flow is then divided by the interest expense to produce the interest coverage ratio. (So, interest coverage equals EBIT / interest expense.) A firm with a low interest coverage ratio runs the risk of being unable to cover its interest payments (that is, defaulting on its debt). Therefore, this ratio also shows the degree of flexibility a firm has to bear negative events (which decrease EBIT) without defaulting on its debt or having to cut back on its operations in some way. For ABC, interest coverage is equal to $806 million (their earnings from operations) divided by $58 million (their interest expense), or 13.9 for 2013.

2.5.3 *Liquidity Ratios*

The two liquidity ratios listed in Figure 2.7 both provide information about the level of cash the firm has on hand, so they are indicators of the short-term financial situation of a firm.

The current ratio is the value of current assets to the value of current liabilities. It indicates the ability of a firm to cover its current obligations, such as payments to employees and to suppliers, using the assets that it would be able to convert into cash in the short term. A low current ratio could raise questions about whether a firm would be able to pay off its short-run obligations at a given point in time. Calculating for ABC, we divide the $4.3 billion in current assets by the $4.2 billion in current liabilities, generating a ratio of 1.0. This level suggests that the firm would be just able to cover its current obligations using current assets in the worst-case scenario where all the current obligations came due right away.

The quick ratio is similar to the current ratio, but subtracts inventory from current assets in the numerator of the ratio. Inventory is removed because liquidating inventory quickly may be difficult for certain types of inventory (spare airplane parts, for example), especially in comparison to the other components of current assets, such as cash and accounts receivable. For ABC, this ratio is 0.86, suggesting that, if unable to quickly convert inventory into cash, ABC would not be able to cover its current obligations with current assets if the current obligations all came due right away.

2.5.4 Turnover and the Cash Cycle

The last set of ratios provided in Figure 2.7 are all measures of "turnover." Broadly speaking, they all show the speed with which a firm proceeds through its sales cycle.

The payables period shows the number of days it takes for a firm to pay its suppliers for inputs and other things that it purchases to produce the goods or services that it sells. The formula for the payables period, shown in Figure 2.7, divides accounts payable from the balance sheet by the average purchases per day by the firm, which is calculated by dividing the total purchases over the previous year by 365.[10] This ratio provides a measure of how long on average a firm takes to pay its suppliers. For ABC, we can calculate this ratio by dividing $1.2 billion in accounts payable by a total cost of goods sold of $8.1 billion. The total cost of goods sold comes from adding the cost of products and the cost of services on the income statement. We don't include other entries under Costs and Expenses on the income statement (such as financing interest or research and development) because these entries do not represent costs directly related to the materials needed to produce the products (goods and services) that it sells. For ABC, the payables period is 55 days, which means that it takes an average of 55 days from the time an invoice comes in from a vendor before a payment is made to that vendor. In general, a high payables period may be interpreted as good or bad. It can be good in that it allows the firm to preserve cash by taking longer to pay suppliers. However, a high payables period may also be an indicator of financial trouble at a firm because it is having trouble generating cash quick enough to pay suppliers on a timely basis.

Inventory days is a measure of the average number of days that goods and products sit in inventory at a firm. The inventory value from the balance sheet is divided by the average cost of goods sold per day, which is calculated by taking the cost of goods sold over the last year and dividing by 365. For ABC, we can calculate this ratio by dividing $624 million in inventory by a total cost of goods sold of $8.1 billion, yielding 28 inventory days. A higher number of inventory days suggests that products sit in inventory a long time (thus increasing inventory costs) before being sold. In general, a lower inventory days measure indicates greater efficiency in the operations of a firm.

Finally, the collection period indicates the average number of days that it takes a firm to receive payment for goods sold to its customers. The collection period is calculated by taking the accounts receivable at a firm and dividing by the average sales per day. This measure is an indicator of how efficient a firm is at getting paid from its customers. The higher the collection period is for a firm, the longer it takes for the firm to collect cash from its customers and, therefore, the more financing the firm needs to cover current liabilities until cash is received from its customers. For ABC, this indicator is 52 days: $1.5 billion divided by $10.6 billion over 365, or about 52 days. Interestingly, the time that it takes ABC to collect money for goods sold is about 3 days shorter than the number of days that it takes ABC to pay its own suppliers. This is a good thing because it means the firm is essentially using its suppliers to finance the receivables from its customers.[11]

These three turnover ratios—payables period, inventory days, and collection period—together indicate the *cash cycle* of a firm, as follows:

Inventory Days + Collection Period – Payables Period = Cash Cycle (3)

The cash cycle indicates the number of days for which cash is tied up in the production and sales process. In other words, once a dollar of cash goes out of the firm, the cash cycle is a measure of how long it takes for the dollar to come back into the firm. All else equal, a lower value for the cash cycle indicates more efficient use of cash. For ABC, the cash cycle is 25 days.

2.5.5 The Dupont Formula

The Dupont formula provides insight to the ways in which a firm generates its returns. The formula itself is[12]

Return on Equity = Profit Margin × Asset Turnover × Leverage   (4)

$$\frac{\text{Net Income}}{\text{Equity}} = \frac{\text{Net Income}}{\text{Revenue}} \times \frac{\text{Revenue}}{\text{Assets}} \times \frac{\text{Assets}}{\text{Equity}} \qquad (5)$$

It shows that a firm's ultimate goal—return on equity (ROE)—arises from the profit margin, asset turnover, and leverage.[13] A higher profit margin boosts ROE because it means that every dollar of sales translates into higher net earnings. Asset turnover indicates the degree to which assets are deployed to generate sales. It indicates to what extent the assets of a firm are converted into sales, the source of potential earnings—a higher ratio indicates greater effectiveness at converting assets into sales. Finally, higher leverage translates into higher ROE because higher leverage indicates lower stockholder equity relative to assets. Using the Dupont formula allows you to break down and analyze the factors driving a firm's ROE.

For ABC, we can take the ratios calculated earlier and use those to illustrate the Dupont formula:

$11\% = 6\% \times 0.80 \times 2.34$

For ABC, the source of its ROE appears to be heavily weighted toward leverage. However, interpreting the sources of ROE must be done in the context of the firm's particular industry, as well as the firm's stage in its own life cycle. For example, we might expect that a young, growing firm might generate ROE relatively more via leverage, as compared to a large, mature firm.

2.6 Financial Distress

A firm in financial distress runs the risk of no longer being able to remain an operating entity. Two numbers in the balance sheet, along with their counterparts in the income statement and cash flow statements, can provide important information about a firm's financial health. First, low cash balances, along with a negative cash flow, could indicate trouble. Cash provides the flexibility to deal with surprises and to ensure ready access to materials needed for doing business. A string of negative cash flow results translates into declining cash balances on the balance sheet, implying reduced ability of the firm to optimize its operations. For this reason, paying close attention to financial ratios that deal with the cash account and liquidity is important in assessing the level of financial distress a firm might be under.

The other important number to look to for signs of financial distress is the value of stockholders' equity, along with the net income results. Stockholders' equity shows the net worth of the firm, and a firm with negative net worth may be essentially bankrupt. A string of negative net income results feeding into stockholders' equity may be a signal of financial distress. For this reason, paying close attention to financial ratios dealing with the equity account is an important part of assessing the level of financial distress a firm might be under.

Endnotes

1 Another common way to think about this is that the income and cash flow statements provide the information that causes the balance sheet to change from one period of time to the next.

2 Quite often in practice, when someone is speaking about equity capital, the speaker will refer to it as simply *capital* for short. We will be precise when discussing capital in this book, referring to it as either *debt capital* or *equity capital*.

3 Other factors also affect shareholders' equity, so the change in shareholders' equity from one year to the next might not exactly equal net income for the year. Information on the universe of transactions that determine the changes in shareholders' equity from one year to the next is recorded in the consolidated statements of stockholders' equity. For U.S. public companies, these are available from the U.S. Securities and Exchange Commission, at www.sec.gov.

4 Due to rounding, the difference between these numbers is $86 million.

5 The reason for this is that cash cannot be created out of nothing, nor can it simply disappear. All cash has to be generated and used up by the accounts on a balance sheet.

6 Note that we have computed ROE here by dividing 2013 net income by the end of year 2013 shareholders' equity. Another common way that ROE is calculated is to divide 2013 net income by beginning of year 2013 shareholders' equity (which is equal to the end of year 2012 equity).

7 Note that, all else equal, a given level of earnings produces a higher ROE if the right-hand side of the balance sheet has more debt relative to equity, simply because the denominator of the ratio will decline. This is also the result of leverage. The higher the leverage a firm has, the greater the risk, and therefore, the greater the potential return on its shareholders' investments into the firm.

8 Another way to think about this is that the fewer assets a firm has to carry to generate a certain amount of revenue, the more efficient that firm must be and the more profitable that firm will be from an ROA and ROE perspective.

9 If we flip this ratio around to equity divided by assets, this new ratio has a commonly used name: *equity ratio*. Note that the debt ratio plus the equity ratio always equals 1.

10 Sometimes a firm may not separately report purchases on its income statement or the footnotes. In this case, it is common to use cost of goods sold as a substitute for purchases in calculating the payables period.

11 Another way to state this is that the firm is using its suppliers to finance its customers.

12 In this case, we define *leverage* as the ratio of assets to equity. Note that because assets – equity = liabilities, this ratio tells us about the leverage of the firm. A high ratio implies relatively high assets relative to equity, thus relatively high liabilities and thus leverage. A low ratio implies relatively low assets relative to equity, and thus relatively low liabilities and low leverage.

13 Recall that ROE can be measured using the beginning of year equity or end of year equity. Either approach is valid with this formula as long as it is consistently applied. So, if beginning of year equity is used to measure ROE, beginning of year equity and beginning of year assets must also be used to measure leverage and asset turnover.

3

Financial Forecasting

3.1 Introduction

As we stated in Chapter 1, "Introduction," the objective of this book is to develop a set of valuation frameworks that will enable a business manager to quantify the value implications of business decisions. Those business decisions can range from building a new manufacturing facility to developing a new product to acquiring a firm.

The foundation of all valuation frameworks in finance is the present value relation:

$$Value_0 = \frac{E(CF_1)}{1+r} + \frac{E(CF_2)}{(1+r)^2} + \frac{E(CF_3)}{(1+r)^3} + ... \tag{1}$$

Here, $E(CF_1)$, $E(CF_2)$, and so on are expected future cash flows, r denotes a discount rate, and $Value_0$ is the value of the project that we are trying to measure. There are two key pieces of information needed to evaluate this present value relation and measure the value implication of a business decision. The first is the expected future cash flows that would result from the decision. The second is the discount rate, which reflects the riskiness of the future cash flows (and, therefore, the risk entailed in the decision), which is used to discount the expected future cash flows and transform them into a value amount today.

We will begin by developing a method to determine expected future cash flows. As mentioned in Chapter 1, any project can be put in the context of a balance sheet. In fact, the project can be thought of as a series of balance sheets, with each one representing the state of the project at a different point in time. As you learned in Chapter 2, "Financial Statement Analysis," the change from one balance sheet to the next can be captured in an income statement, a cash flow statement, and/or a sources and uses of cash statement. Therefore, the project can be thought of as a series of balance sheets, income statements, and different types of cash flow statements. To evaluate Equation 1, we need to develop expected future cash flows. The obvious place to calculate them is from the series of balance sheets, income statements, and especially the cash flow statements that represent the business decision. In this chapter, we explain how to develop these future, or projected, financial statements. We specifically focus in this chapter on how to develop these projected financial statements for a business, but keep in mind that the techniques described here will work for any type of business decision.

So, in this chapter, you will learn how to project a firm's financial statements into the future. We explain projections for growth of the entire firm and how to plan the launch of a new project. We will continue using the example of ABC Company to illustrate precisely how financial forecasts are put together.

3.2 Constructing Pro Forma Financials

Firms need to plan for the future. Plans need to be made both for the overall growth path of the firm and for new initiatives that may be launched. Looking into the future is necessarily difficult because it inherently involves a great deal of uncertainty. However, recognizing this uncertainty and making logical and well-reasoned assumptions about likely outcomes allows the firm to deal intelligently with the need to plan for the future.

A firm constructs pro forma financials to project financial conditions into the future. In the most basic sense, *pro forma financials* are the balance sheet and income statements extended out for a certain period of time, often five years. Making these projections allows a firm both to see the implications of future growth and to think carefully about how to finance expansion. For example, if a firm wants to grow, it will need to obtain funds for things such as buying inventory, hiring additional employees, and buying or leasing new space if needed. It can get the needed capital by borrowing, issuing equity, or retaining earnings. The pro forma financials give the firm both an idea of the size of the funding needed for future growth and the ways in which those funds could be obtained.

Constructing these statements is fairly straightforward. First, we make assumptions about how certain key components of the financial statement will grow in the future. Second, we extrapolate out the other components of the balance sheet based on our basic assumptions. Finally, we add in a financing path showing where any needed funds will come from. After these basic pieces have been set down, we use some of the financial ratios discussed in the previous chapter to evaluate whether the projected growth path is sustainable. If it is not sustainable, we need to revisit some of the assumptions made in the first step and repeat the projection exercise. If it is sustainable, the firm can use the pro forma financials as a guide for activities and decisions in the near term.

3.2.1 Creating the Pro Forma Worksheet

In this chapter, we'll create pro forma financials for ABC Company, continuing the example that we started in Chapter 2. Figure 3.1 provides the format that we will use. We've split the figure into three parts to make it easier to read. (Figure 3.1a provides explanations of how to calculate the various components of the pro forma financial statement.) We've also combined some of the accounts that appeared in the income statement in Figure 2.4 to streamline the accounts and focus on the most important aspects of putting together our forecast. Indeed, in reality, financial statements are very complex, and each presents aspects unique to each individual firm. Here, we take a high-level view, thus providing an approach applicable to the vast majority of firms.

Figure 3.1.1

	2011	2012	2013	2014	2015	2016	2017	2018
INCOME STATEMENT								
Net Revenue:								
Products	6,171	7,067	7,063	7,769	8,546	9,401	10,341	11,375
Services	3,344	3,401	3,503	3,854	4,239	4,663	5,129	5,642
Financing Income	31	35	37	41	45	50	55	60
Total net revenue	9,546	10,503	10,604	11,664	12,831	14,114	15,525	17,077
Costs and Expenses:								
Cost of products	4,709	5,422	5,431	5,974	6,571	7,228	7,951	8,746
Cost of services	2,555	2,549	2,671	2,938	3,232	3,556	3,911	4,302
Financing interest	27	25	26	28	31	34	37	41
Research and development	235	247	271	298	328	361	397	437
Selling, general and administrative (SGA)	971	1,060	1,122	1,234	1,358	1,494	1,643	1,807
Other expenses	205	243	277	304	335	368	405	445
Total operating expenses (Ln 5 to Ln 13)	8,701	9,546	9,797	10,777	11,855	13,040	14,344	15,779
Earnings from Operations (Ln4-Ln14)	845	957	806	887	976	1,073	1,181	1,299
Interest and other, net	60	42	58	62	66	70	75	80
Earnings before taxes (Ln15-Ln16)	785	915	749	825	910	1,003	1,106	1,218
Provision for taxes	146	184	159	175	193	213	235	259
Net Earnings (Ln17-Ln18)	638	730	590	650	717	790	871	960

BALANCE SHEET

	2011	2012	2013	2014	2015	2016	2017	2018
Current Assets								
Cash and cash equivalents	1,107	911	670	737	811	892	981	1,079
Accounts receivable	1,378	1,540	1,519	1,671	1,838	2,021	2,223	2,446
Financing receivables	223	249	264	290	319	351	386	424
Inventory	511	539	624	687	755	831	914	1,005
Other current assets	1,160	1,277	1,175	1,293	1,422	1,564	1,721	1,893
Total current assets (Lns 20 to 24)	4,378	4,515	4,252	4,677	5,145	5,659	6,225	6,847
Property, plant and equipment	939	980	1,024	1,127	1,239	1,363	1,500	1,650
Long-term financing receivables and other assets	941	1,019	896	986	1,084	1,193	1,312	1,443
Other long-term assets	4,197	5,477	6,975	7,672	8,439	9,283	10,212	11,233
Total assets (Ln25+Lns 26 to 29)	10,455	11,992	13,147	14,462	15,908	17,499	19,249	21,173

Figure 3.1.1 continued

	2011	2012	2013	2014	2015	2016	2017	2018
Liabilities and Stockholders' Equity								
Current Liabilities								
Notes payable and short-term borrowings	154	587	674	741	815	897	986	1,085
Accounts payable	1,234	1,197	1,229	1,352	1,487	1,636	1,800	1,980
Employee compensation and benefits	339	355	333	367	403	444	488	537
Taxes on earnings	76	67	87	96	106	116	128	141
Deferred revenue	515	561	621	683	751	826	909	1,000
Accrued restructuring	92	76	55	60	66	73	80	88
Other accrued liabilities	1,173	1,275	1,205	1,325	1,458	1,604	1,764	1,941
Total current liabilities (Lns 31 to 37)	3,584	4,117	4,204	4,624	5,086	5,595	6,154	6,770
Long-term debt	1,165	1,272	1,879	1,978	2,084	2,200	2,325	2,461
Other liabilities	1,421	1,588	1,460	1,606	1,767	1,943	2,138	2,351
Stockholders' Equity	4,285	5,015	5,604	6,254	6,971	7,761	8,632	9,591
Total liabilities and stockholders' equity	10,455	11,992	13,147	14,462	15,908	17,499	19,249	21,173

Note: All figures are in millions.

Figure 3.1.2

	2011	2012	2013	2014	2015	2016	2017	2018
Rates								
Product revenue growth rate				10.00%	10.00%	10.00%	10.00%	10.00%
Service revenue growth rate				10.00%	10.00%	10.00%	10.00%	10.00%
Financing income revenue growth rate				10.00%	10.00%	10.00%	10.00%	10.00%
Interest rate on borrowing (average)	4.55%	2.26%	2.27%	2.27%	2.27%	2.27%	2.27%	2.27%
Tax rate	18.64%	20.17%	21.24%	21.24%	21.24%	21.24%	21.24%	21.24%
Percentages								
Costs Percentages								
Cost of products/Net revenue from products (NRP)	76.30%	76.73%	76.89%	76.89%	76.89%	76.89%	76.89%	76.89%
Cost of services/Net revenue from services (NRS)	76.41%	74.95%	76.25%	76.25%	76.25%	76.25%	76.25%	76.25%
Financing interest/Financing income (NRF)	86.47%	72.25%	68.15%	68.15%	68.15%	68.15%	68.15%	68.15%
R&D/Total net revenue (TNR)	2.46%	2.35%	2.56%	2.56%	2.56%	2.56%	2.56%	2.56%
SGA/TNR	10.17%	10.09%	10.58%	10.58%	10.58%	10.58%	10.58%	10.58%
Other expenses/TNR	2.15%	2.32%	2.61%	2.61%	2.61%	2.61%	2.61%	2.61%
Total operating expenses/TNR	91.15%	90.89%	92.39%	92.39%	92.39%	92.39%	92.39%	92.39%

Figure 3.1.2 continued

	2011	2012	2013	2014	2015	2016	2017	2018
Assets Percentages								
Cash/Total net revenue (TNR)	11.59%	8.67%	6.32%	6.32%	6.32%	6.32%	6.32%	6.32%
Accounts receivable/TNR	14.44%	14.66%	14.32%	14.32%	14.32%	14.32%	14.32%	14.32%
Financing receivables/TNR	2.34%	2.37%	2.48%	2.48%	2.48%	2.48%	2.48%	2.48%
Inventory/TNR	5.35%	5.13%	5.89%	5.89%	5.89%	5.89%	5.89%	5.89%
Other Current Assets/TNR	12.15%	12.16%	11.08%	11.08%	11.08%	11.08%	11.08%	11.08%
Property, Plant, and Equipment/TNR	9.83%	9.33%	9.66%	9.66%	9.66%	9.66%	9.66%	9.66%
LT Financing Receivables/TNR	9.85%	9.70%	8.45%	8.45%	8.45%	8.45%	8.45%	8.45%
Other long-term assets/TNR	43.97%	52.15%	65.78%	65.78%	65.78%	65.78%	65.78%	65.78%
Liabilities Percentages								
Short-term borrowings/TNR	1.61%	5.59%	6.35%	6.35%	6.35%	6.35%	6.35%	6.35%
Accounts Payable/Total net revenue (TNR)	12.93%	11.40%	11.59%	11.59%	11.59%	11.59%	11.59%	11.59%
Employee compensation & ben/TNR	3.55%	3.38%	3.14%	3.14%	3.14%	3.14%	3.14%	3.14%
Deferred revenue/TNR	5.40%	5.34%	5.85%	5.85%	5.85%	5.85%	5.85%	5.85%
Accrued restructuring/TNR	0.97%	0.72%	0.51%	0.51%	0.51%	0.51%	0.51%	0.51%
Other accrued liabilities/TNR	12.28%	12.14%	11.36%	11.36%	11.36%	11.36%	11.36%	11.36%
Other liabilities/TNR	14.89%	15.12%	13.77%	13.77%	13.77%	13.77%	13.77%	13.77%
Taxes on earnings/TNR	0.79%	0.64%	0.82%	0.82%	0.82%	0.82%	0.82%	0.82%

Figure 3.1.3

Ratios	2011	2012	2013	2014	2015	2016	2017	2018
Return on equity (ROE)	14.90%	14.56%	10.52%	10.39%	10.28%	10.18%	10.09%	10.00%
Return on assets (ROA)	6.11%	6.09%	4.48%	4.49%	4.51%	4.51%	4.52%	4.53%
Profit margin	6.69%	6.95%	5.56%	5.57%	5.59%	5.60%	5.61%	5.62%
Leverage	12.62%	15.50%	19.42%	18.80%	18.22%	17.69%	17.20%	16.75%
EBIT (Earnings before interest and taxes)	845	957	806	887	976	1,073	1,181	1,299
EBIT/Sales	8.85%	9.11%	7.61%	7.61%	7.61%	7.61%	7.61%	7.61%
Inventory turnover	14.22	14.79	12.98	12.98	12.98	12.98	12.98	12.98
Interest coverage	14.06	22.73	13.92	14.38	14.84	15.28	15.72	16.14
Collection period	52.69	53.52	52.28	52.28	52.28	52.28	52.28	52.28
Inventory days	25.66	24.67	28.12	28.12	28.12	28.12	28.12	28.12
Payables period	62.01	54.81	55.38	55.38	55.38	55.38	55.38	55.38

Figure 3.1a Financial Forecasting—The Components of the Financial Statement

Component	Projection Method
	Income Statement Components
Net Revenue from Products (NRP)	Assumed rate of growth
Net Revenue from Services (NRS)	Assumed rate of growth
Total Net Revenue (TNR)	Sum of projected revenues from products, services, and financing
Cost of Products	NPR Projection $* \dfrac{\text{Cost of Products}}{\text{NRP}}$ from previous year
Cost of Services	NRS Projection $* \dfrac{\text{Cost of Services}}{\text{NRS}}$ from previous year
R&D Expenses	TNR Projection $* \dfrac{\text{R\&D}}{\text{TNR}}$ from previous year
Selling, General, and Admin. (SGA)	TNR Projection $* \dfrac{\text{SGA}}{\text{TNR}}$ from previous year
Interest and other, net	$\dfrac{\text{Interest and other, net}}{\text{Short-term borrowings + Long-term debt}}$ from previous year
Provision for taxes	$\dfrac{\text{Provision for taxes}}{\text{Earnings before taxes}}$ from previous year
	Balance Sheet Components
Cash and cash equivalents	TNR Projection $* \dfrac{\text{Cash}}{\text{TNR}}$ from previous year
Accounts Receivable	TNR Projection $* \dfrac{\text{Accounts Receivable}}{\text{TNR}}$ from previous year
Inventory	TNR Projection $* \dfrac{\text{Inventory}}{\text{TNR}}$ from previous year
Property, Plant, and Equip. (PPE)	TNR Projection $* \dfrac{\text{PPE}}{\text{TNR}}$ from previous year
Accounts Payable	TNR Projection $* \dfrac{\text{Accounts Payable}}{\text{TNR}}$ from previous year

Component	Projection Method
Stockholders' Equity (SE)	Stockholders' Equity from previous year + Net Earnings from current year
Notes payable and short-term borrowings	$\text{TNR Projection} * \dfrac{\text{Notes Payable and Short-Term Borrowings}}{\text{TNR}}$ from previous year
Long-term debt	Amount needed to "bridge the gap" left over when subtracting SE and other liabilities from total assets

Source: Authors.

The numbers in the first three columns of Figure 3.1.1 are identical to those in the balance sheet and income statement tables in Chapter 2, but they are reorganized in a way that will be useful for constructing the pro forma financial statements. Both the income statement and balance sheet are combined here so that the link between the two financial statements is very clear as we create financial projections.

In Figures 3.1.2 and 3.1.3 are three new sections. The top section of Figure 3.1.2 contains a set of rates that are our assumptions about the future growth of ABC. The bottom half shows a set of percentages that will be used for constructing the individual pieces of the financial forecast. Figure 3.1.3 contains many of the financial ratios from Chapter 2; these will be used to evaluate the strengths and weaknesses of our planned path for growth.

3.2.2 Rates

The section in Figure 3.1.2 titled Rates contains the key assumptions for making a financial forecast. The top three lines show some important assumptions about the future growth path of ABC. They set out the assumptions we'll make about the rate of growth of revenue from products, services, and financing, respectively. Based on the future revenue forecasts calculated from these assumptions, we are able to project out the other components of the income statement and balance sheet, such as costs of products and services, accounts payable, and accounts receivable.

In Figure 3.1.2, we've assumed a growth rate of 10% in all three areas. The choice of a reasonable rate of growth is a critical element of putting together pro forma financials. The target should be guided both by knowledge of market conditions and by the sustainability of growth at a given target level (as discussed later in this chapter).

This assumed 10% rate of growth will be used to project our future net revenue. For example, the 2014 net revenue shown in Figure 3.1.1 is calculated by multiplying the 2013 net revenue of $10.6 billion by 10% and then adding that number to the 2013 revenue. Restating:

2014 Total Net Revenue =
2013 Total Net Revenue + 2013 Total Net Revenue $\circ$ 10% (2)

or

$11.7 billion = $10.6 billion + $10.6 billion $\circ$ 10%   (3)

The Rates section of Figure 3.1.2 also contains assumptions about interest rates on any borrowings and taxes on income. These rates are used to calculate projected interest expenses and tax payments. For the purposes of this example, the tax rate in Figure 3.1.2 comes from dividing the provision for taxes from the income statement ($159 million for 2013) by the earnings before taxes ($749 million for 2013). This ratio provides an average tax rate for ABC. In reality, any multinational pays taxes in many different countries at many different rates. Within the firm itself, one could use this more detailed information to calculate the provision for taxes more precisely. For the purposes of our pro forma financial statements, however, the rough average provides useful guidance about how much in taxes ABC will need to pay.

The assumption on the interest rate in Figure 3.1.2 is also a rough estimate. Note that ABC's balance sheet shows both "Notes payable and short-term borrowings" and "Long-term debt." In reality, any firm pays a range of interest rates on its various borrowings, depending on things such as the source of the funds and the maturity of the debt. For the purposes of our pro forma financial statements, we calculated the interest rate by dividing the "Interest and other, net" from the income statement ($58 million in 2013) by the total amount of debt on ABC's balance sheet ($2.5 billion for 2013). Internally, a firm has more detailed information on interest rates and debt structure and would be able to provide a more precise estimate. For the purposes of this example, we will use the rough estimate of 2.27% shown in Figure 3.1.2.

3.2.3 Percentages

The Percentages section of Figure 3.1.2 of the pro forma worksheet shows the relationship among certain elements of the financial statements; these percentages will be used to estimate the magnitude of these individual accounts in our financial projections. For most entries, we calculate the share of the individual entry in total revenue. (Recall that total revenue is composed of the sum of revenue from products, services, and financing.)

For example, as Figure 3.1.2 shows, selling, general, and administrative (SGA) costs were about 10% of total revenue in 2011, 2012, and 2013. (See the line labeled SGA/TNR in the section labeled Costs Percentages.) As an example, this number is calculated for 2013 by dividing SGA costs for 2013 ($1.1 billion) by total revenue for 2013 ($10.6 billion), yielding the 10.58% shown in Figure 3.1.2. As another example, cash holdings were about 12% of total net revenue in 2011, 9% in 2012, and 6% in 2013. (See the line labeled Cash/Total net revenue in the section labeled Assets Percentages.) For 2013, we can make this calculation by dividing cash of $670 million by total net revenue of $10.6 billion, which comes to 6.32%, as shown in Figure 3.1.2. In most cases, we use these percentages to estimate the value of different entries in future financial statements by simply assuming a constant relationship between an individual component of the income statement or balance sheet and net revenue. For example, we will project that SGA costs will be about 10% of total revenue in the years in our pro forma financial statement, based on the 10% of revenue that it held in 2011, 2012, and 2013. This makes sense because SGA costs include things such as human resources and marketing activities that would be expected to increase with the value of revenue. Therefore, once we assume a growth rate for total revenue, it is straightforward to figure out the value of SGA and many other entries on the financial statements (see Figure 3.1.2).

As a specific example, we can calculate SGA expenses for 2014 by multiplying 10.58% by 2014 net revenue of $11.7 billion, yielding SGA expenses of $1.2 billion for 2014. Restating:

2014 SGA Expenses =
2014 Total Net Revenue * 10.58%   (4)

or

$1.2 billion = $11.7 billion * 10.58%   (5)

If you recall the way that we calculated net revenue for 2014 and the SGA percent in total net revenue, we can further break down these numbers to show how they are derived from the 2013 financial statements (where TNR stands for total net revenue):

$$2014 \text{ SGA Expenses} = [2013 \text{ TNR} + 2013 \text{ TNR} \times 10\%] \times \frac{2013 \text{ SGA Expenses}}{2013 \text{ TNR}} \quad (6)$$

$$\$1.2 \text{ billion} = [\$10.6 \text{ billion} + \$10.6 \text{ billion} \times \frac{\$1.1 \text{ billion}}{\$10.6 \text{ billion}} \quad (7)$$

We use this same method (that is, as a percentage of the forecasted net revenue) for penciling in a number for property, plant, and equipment (PPE). However, note that PPE numbers reported on the balance sheet are often net of depreciation. There is a calculation made before entering the net PPE number on the balance sheet. We discuss this topic further in a later chapter.

For some entries, we need to use the subcomponents of total revenue (that is, revenue from products, services, or financing). For example, to calculate the cost of products, we will use the cost of products from the previous year as a percentage of net revenue *from products* for that year, rather than as a percent of total revenue. In Figure 3.1.2, ABC's cost of products as a percent of net revenue from products was about 77% in 2013, and we'll use that same percentage to project out the cost of products as a percent of revenue from products into the future. (See the line labeled Cost of products/Net revenue from products in the section labeled Costs Percentages.)

$$2014 \text{ Cost of Products} =$$
$$2014 \text{ Net Revenue from Products } °76.89 \tag{8}$$

or

$$\$6.0 \text{ billion} = \$7.8 \text{ billion} ° 76.89\% \tag{9}$$

Similarly, we will use the cost of services as a percentage of net revenue *from services* (about 76% in 2013) to pencil in numbers for a future cost of services as a percentage of net revenue from services. The relevant calculation is

$$2014 \text{ Cost of Services} =$$
$$2014 \text{ Net Revenue from Services } °76.25 \tag{10}$$

or

$$\$2.9 \text{ billion} = \$3.9 \text{ billion} ° 76.25\% \tag{11}$$

Thus, we use such percentages to calculate the cost of products and cost of services in future years, based on the net revenue from products and from services in these future years.

More generally, we make our projections by assuming that the relationship between other accounts (for example, accounts receivable or accounts payable), and total net revenue remains at the 2013 level for the next five years. Thus, such a ratio ($1.5 billion divided by $10.6 billion or 14.32% for accounts receivable; $1.2 billion divided by $10.6 billion or 11.59% for accounts receivable) is maintained throughout the five years of the forecast.

Such an assumption is not unreasonable because that ratio varied little over the three years of information that we have available. Another assumption that could be used instead would be to take an average of the last three years. Alternatively, if we had additional information that suggested that the relationship between cost of products and net revenue from products were likely to change in the near future (maybe we expected to receive steep discounts on inputs for the next couple of years), we could use that additional information to predict the future relationship between costs and net revenues.

3.2.4 Stockholders' Equity

As discussed in Chapter 2, stockholders' equity represents the net worth of the firm; it is, by definition, the excess of assets over liabilities. Year by year, it fluctuates in accordance with how well the firm does. If a firm is profitable (that is, if net earnings are positive), stockholders' equity will likely increase. If a firm had negative net earnings, equity will likely fall. We will use this relationship for projecting equity in our pro forma financial statements.

As a first pass, we will assume that net earnings from a given year flow directly into equity for that year. If the firm had positive earnings in a given year, equity will increase by exactly that amount. For example, referring to Figure 3.1.1, in our 2014 financial forecast, ABC's $650 million of net earnings in 2014 are assumed to flow directly into the 2014 value of stockholders' equity. (Recall that the balance sheet is constructed at the end of the year, whereas the income statement reflects activities over the course of the year. So, the income earned during the course of 2014 shows up in the balance sheet at the end of 2014.)

In reality, of course, the destination of net earnings is more complex. The firm could issue dividends, thereby returning some of the earnings to shareholders. It could also buy back shares, thereby making all outstanding shares more valuable. For our purposes, we will assume that all net earnings flow through into equity (that is, are *retained earnings*).

3.2.5 Calculating Projected Financial Shortfalls

After we have completed the pro forma income statement and all nondebt portions of the balance sheet, we can figure out projected financial shortfalls. A relationship from Chapter 2 shows our method for calculating these shortfalls:

Assets = Liabilities + Shareholders' Equity   (12)

This relationship is important because it shows how to calculate the remaining pieces of the pro forma financial statements.

Thus far, we have calculated assets, shareholders' equity, and some types of liabilities on the pro forma balance sheet. To calculate the remaining piece of the balance sheet (debt), we can expand the earlier equation:

Assets =
[Debt = Other Liabilities] + Shareholders' Equity   (13)

Rearranging the equation, we find that

Debt =
Assets – Shareholders' Equity – Other Liabilities   (14)

Therefore, we simply calculate debt as the difference between assets, shareholders' equity, and the other liabilities that we have already included in the pro forma financial statement.

3.2.5.1 Debt

For the case of ABC, our 2014 balance sheet forecast shows total assets of $14.5 billion and stockholders' equity of $6.3 billion. To calculate Other Liabilities, we need to sum up the nondebt pieces of the Liabilities section of the balance sheet. For ABC, these entries include accounts payable, employee compensation and benefits, taxes on earnings, deferred revenue, accrued restructuring, other accrued liabilities, and other liabilities. Taken together, these elements sum to $6.2 billion if we include short-term borrowings, and $5.5 billion if we do not include short-term borrowings. (We explain later the importance of this distinction.) Thus, assuming we include short-term borrowings in Other Liabilities, we can calculate the projected financial shortfall as $2.0 billion by subtracting shareholders' equity and other liabilities from total assets. So, ABC needs to borrow $2 billion in total in the first year (2014) to sustain the pace of growth we are projecting. Intuitively, this calculation follows directly from the most basic rule about financial statements: that balance sheets must balance.

One additional complication is that there are several ways to borrow funds. In the case of ABC, one account on the balance sheet is "Notes payable and short-term borrowings" and another is "Long-term debt." The needed debt could fall into either category. For the purposes of the exercise here, we assumed that short-term borrowings continue at the same percent of total net revenue as in 2013, implying that short-term debt in 2014 will be in the amount of $741 million. (This number is calculated by multiplying the ratio for short-term borrowings to net revenue that we have assumed for our forecast [6.35%] by our projected level of net revenue for 2014 [$11.7 billion].) Subtracting this amount of short-term debt from the amount of total debt needed, as we did earlier by including short-term with other liabilities, will give us the amount of long-term debt needed to finance this project. Based on our growth projection, ABC's projected long-term debt for 2014 is about $2 billion. Essentially, long-term debt bridges the gap between assets and equity plus other liabilities (in this case, including short-term debt).

3.2.5.2 Interest Expenses

Now that we know the magnitude of debt, we can calculate the "Interest and other, net" category in the income statement. To do so, we simply multiply the interest rate in the Rates section in Figure 3.1.2 of our pro forma worksheet (2.27%) by the magnitude of both short-term and long-term debt. Doing so, we can see that interest costs are estimated to run to $62 million for 2014.

As a final point here, note that there is an inherent circularity to generating projections of interest expenses. To calculate 2014 interest expenses, we need to know 2014 levels of short-term and long-term debt. However, as noted earlier

Debt =
Assets – Shareholders' Equity – Other Liabilities   (15)

However, to calculate debt, we must know interest expenses because interest expenses are used to calculate net earnings, which in turn flow into shareholders' equity. (See Section 2.4, "Market Value Balance Sheets," where we assumed that net earnings from a given year flow directly into equity for that year.) Thus, debt (because it is calculated using shareholders' equity) and interest expenses must be simultaneously calculated. There are methods that can be used to make these calculations.[1] An alternative way of generating an estimate for interest expenses is to take the debt level from the previous year (2013, in this case) and multiplying this debt level by the assumed interest rate. (For ABC, this would give us approximately: $2.5 billion ° 2.27% = $58 million.) In reality, interest expenses are generated by the level of debt throughout the year, rather than by the level of debt at either the beginning (as shown, in this case, by the 2013 balance sheet) or end of the year (as shown, in this case, by the 2014 balance sheet). Therefore, this alternative approach is also reasonable.

3.3 Bridging Financial Shortfalls

Earlier, we assumed that the funding needed for expansion (that is, the financial shortfall) would come from debt. The gap between assets and other liabilities plus shareholders' equity was bridged by borrowing. In reality, there are other ways to acquire funding. For example, a firm could issue equity, which would also bring in cash. Issuing equity has the downside of diluting the value of existing shares, but it also allows the firm to avoid future interest and principal payments. Alternatively, a firm could potentially sell some nonessential assets to generate funding.

An additional point to keep in mind is that the method that a firm uses to fund growth and the magnitude of the funding required are critical measures of whether a growth target is realistic. If the financial projection shows that a firm will be increasing borrowing every year into the foreseeable future, the firm likely will not be able to maintain the planned pace of expansion. We return to this point later in the chapter.

3.4 Financial Ratios

Figure 3.1.3 of the pro forma worksheet shows a number of the ratios introduced in Chapter 2. We can use the path over time of these ratios to evaluate a given growth path. Before evaluating the path, however, a firm needs to think about its goals for the future. Does it want to increase return on equity? By how much? How much debt is it willing to take on? After these decisions are made, ratio analysis shows the impact of a given growth strategy.

3.4.1 Performance Ratios

The first three ratios in Figure 3.1.3 provide information about a firm's overall performance. Return on equity (ROE), return on assets (ROA), and profit margin all show the degree to which the firm is generating returns to investors. At the most basic level, a plan for growth should generate ROE, ROA, and a profit margin at least comparable to industry peers. If the plan does not generate growth at that level, it suggests that the plan is likely not worth pursuing and that obtaining financing for the plan is likely to be difficult.

We see that ABC had an ROE of 11% in 2013; our plans for 10% growth per year indicate an ROE that is around 10% in the first year, and then stays fairly flat throughout the forecast, ending up at around 10% ROE in 2018. The ROA is projected to remain fairly flat at around 4.5%. Therefore, this growth path essentially keeps the firm at around the same performance level as it had in 2013. For investors looking for stability, this plan may be attractive; however, it does not promise greater returns through the forecast period.

3.4.2 Leverage Ratios

One important decision variable for a path of growth is the degree to which a firm takes on debt. The leverage ratios show the extent to which expansion needs to be financed by borrowing. The leverage ratio shows the ratio of total borrowings to asset; a growing leverage ratio may be a cause for concern, a point that we return to in the next section. Our growth path for ABC shows a gradual decline in leverage, with a leverage ratio of 19% in 2014 steadily decreasing to 17% in 2018. From the leverage perspective, this growth path does not appear to raise any concerns.

The interest coverage, or net earnings before taxes minus interest expense divided by interest expense (see Figure 2.7), provides an indication of whether the firm will be able to handle any increased leverage associated with a growth plan. For ABC, the interest coverage ratio increases over the horizon of the forecast, growing from 14 in 2014 to 16 in 2018. Because an increasing ratio implies that income available to pay interest expenses will rise relative to those interest payments, this path for interest coverage indicates that covering interest payments would become increasingly less burdensome over the course of the forecast. Again, this ratio does not raise any red flags about the feasibility of this projected growth path.

3.5 Sustainable Growth

We can think about the sustainable level of growth in two ways. First, in the long run, a firm will not be able to grow at a faster pace than the rate of growth in returns to equity. Recall the expression we used earlier:

Assets = Liabilities + Shareholders' Equity

Assets = Debt + Other Liabilities + Shareholders' Equity

Shareholders' Equity = Assets − Debt − Other Liabilities

This relationship is also illustrated in Figure 3.2. In the example in the figure, we assume that sales grow at 10%. Based on our assumptions about growth in assets (and also nondebt liabilities), this means that either debt or stockholders' equity must grow to match the expansion in the right side of the balance sheet. A firm would not be able to maintain a constant increase in debt with no end in sight for borrowing, because a lender would not be willing to extend funds indefinitely. To maintain a certain level of growth in assets, therefore, a firm must grow at a pace no greater than the growth rate of the return on equity, because this number represents the increase in the shareholders' equity portion of the balance sheet. In other words

Maximum Sustainable Growth Rate = Return on Equity

In Figure 3.2, the ROE must be at least 10% for that pace of growth to be sustainable.

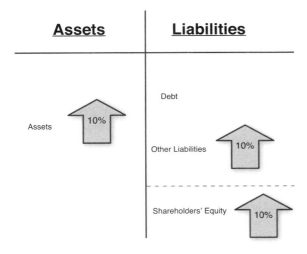

Growth in sales = 10%

Figure 3.2 Illustration of sustainable growth

An alternative way to think about the sustainable level of growth is to focus on the leverage ratio. A leverage ratio that increases each year of a forecast raises red flags about whether the planned path is actually feasible. A constantly increasing debt ratio indicates that a firm's growth is based on higher and higher debt as a percent of assets. In other words, debt is increasing faster than assets. This path would not be feasible as a long-term path.

Returning to Figure 3.1, we can analyze whether our proposed growth path for ABC is sustainable. The ratios in Figure 3.1.3 show, first, that the projected ROE hovers around 10% over the five-year projection. With ROE around the same level as the planned growth in revenue, this path does appear sustainable, and does not raise any obvious concerns, just as we concluded in our earlier discussion of the declining leverage ratio and the increasing interest coverage. Thus, both of these approaches indicate that our planned growth of 10% per year is sustainable, although it is below the maximum sustainable growth rate.

Endnote

1 If these calculations are made using Microsoft Excel, Excel Calculation Preferences must be set to Limit Iterations. If this setting is different, an error message will result stating that Excel is not able to calculate the formula because it contains a circular reference.

4

Free Cash Flows

4.1 Introduction

As stated in Chapter 1, "Introduction," the main goal of this book is to figure out a detailed methodology for measuring the value of any business decision, project, or asset. What this essentially means is that we need to be able to evaluate the following present value relation for any business decision, project, or asset:

$$Value_0 = \frac{E(CF_1)}{1+r} + \frac{E(CF_2)}{(1+r)^2} + \frac{E(CF_3)}{(1+r)^3} + \dots \qquad (1)$$

where $E(CF_1)$, $E(CF_2)$, and so on are expected future cash flows, r denotes a discount rate, and $Value_0$ is the value today (time 0) of the project that we are trying to measure. Because all the cash flows and discount rates are expectations of future events, in the previous chapter we started the process of determining these expectations by figuring out how to project financial statements into the future. In this chapter, you learn how to use these projected financial statements to determine the numerators of Equation 1.

4.2 Free Cash Flow Definition

Chapter 3, "Financial Forecasting," showed that as a balance sheet and income statement are projected for a business, we cannot automatically meet both of our goals of having financial statements that match our business objectives and having the balance sheet balance. Meeting business objectives means projecting the left-hand side of the balance sheet (the business operations) and the income statement in a way that achieves the specific goals of revenue growth, profitability, and asset turnover that we desire or expect. However, this leaves out an important variable: the right-hand side of the balance sheet. Leaving this out results in the balance sheet being unbalanced in our projections. Essentially what we learn from this is that the financing of the operations must also be considered as an integrated component in business objectives. Any business plan has a financing implication, and the financing implication will then determine whether that business plan is feasible. Therefore, the two go hand in hand, and any projections of the left-hand side of the balance sheet must incorporate a financing component that will allow the left-hand and right-hand sides of the balance sheet to match and therefore make the balance sheet balance.

In Chapter 3, as we projected the income statement and balance sheet, we set up a "plug" account on the right-hand side of the balance sheet. This allowed us to balance the left-hand and right-hand sides of the balance sheet. For convenience, we considered the plug account as some form of debt; in Figure 3.1, we used long-term debt.[1]

However, the plug can take on any flavor of financing. It could be short-term debt, long-term debt, equity, hybrid equity (such as preferred stock or convertibles), and so on. Therefore, a CFO has to determine not only the amount of financing that a business needs to finance its operations into the future, she must also determine what form this financing should take.[2] In general, the decrease in the financing amount (or plug account) needed each year to balance the left-hand and right-hand sides of the balance sheet is known as *free cash flow*.[3] So, free cash flow is an indication of the amount of unused, or free, cash that is produced by the business. With the way we have been constructing our projected balance sheets so far, this free cash is automatically used to decrease, or pay off, the plug account (long-term debt in the balance sheet projections in Figure 3.1). This is why free cash flow can be measured by how much the plug account decreases.

From the work we have done so far, the free cash flow in any given quarter or year may be calculated as simply the decrease in the plug account on the right-hand side of the balance sheet. Referring back to Figure 3.1, we can examine the long-term debt line of the balance sheet to measure the decrease in the amount of the plug needed to bring the balance sheet into balance. For 2014, this amount was −($1,978M − $1,879M) = −$99M, for 2015 it was −($2,084M − $1,978M) =−$106M, and for 2016, −($2,200M − $2,084M) = −$116M. These negative free cash flows indicate that the business is not projected to produce free cash but instead it is expected to use up cash. As a result of this usage, additional debt has to be issued to raise this extra cash.

4.3 Balance Sheet View of Free Cash Flow

Figure 4.1 shows what free cash flow means. This figure presents the simple balance sheet view of a firm. The left-hand side contains the assets and represents the active business, or operating activities, of the business.[4] The right-hand side represents the financing for the operating activities on the left-hand side. We break down the financing sources into two broad categories: debt and equity.[5] Free cash flow is basically the cash flow that is thrown off by the operating activities of a business and therefore not required for reinvestment back into these operations. As Figure 4.1 shows, the free cash flow is generated on the left-hand side of the balance sheet. Because the cash is no longer needed by the operations, it flows to the right-hand side of the balance sheet. Flowing to the right-hand side essentially means that it is available for distribution back to the original providers of financing for the operating activities of the firm (that is, the investors). If this cash is distributed back to debt holders, it will be in the form of interest and principal repayments. If it is distributed back to equity holders, it will be in the form of dividend payments or share buybacks.

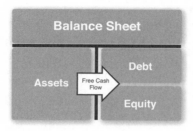

Figure 4.1 Graphical view of the meaning of free cash flow

As we noted in Section 4.2, "Free Cash Flow Definition," free cash flow can also be negative. The free cash flows in ABC's financial projections in Figure 3.1 are negative for 2014 through 2018. Figure 4.2 depicts this situation. Instead of throwing off cash to be distributed by the financing claimants of the firm, the operating activities require further cash investments to meet the required balances to needed for operating activity targets.[6] These cash investments are in addition to any reinvestment of cash that the operations may have generated previously, and therefore it must come from outside investors.

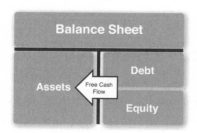

Figure 4.2 Graphical view of free cash flow flowing from RHS to LHS of balance sheet: negative free cash flow

Because the outside investment must be in the form of either debt and/or equity, cash must flow from the debt and equity accounts into operations. Therefore, from a balance sheet standpoint, when free cash flow is negative, cash flows from the right-hand side of the balance sheet to the left-hand side. This cash is then used to finance the operating activities needed to meet business targets.

4.4 Free Cash Flow Calculation: Sources/Uses of Cash

Another, often more intuitive way to think about and calculate free cash flow is to utilize the sources/uses of cash statement, which we discussed in Chapter 2, "Financial Statement Analysis." The sources/uses of cash statement simply looks at every balance sheet account and determines whether that account was a source or a use of cash; i.e., whether the operating activities of the company resulted in that account generating cash or requiring cash.

A sources/uses of cash statement must balance. Because we look at every account on the balance sheet (and balance sheets must balance), the total cash generated by a balance sheet must equal the total cash used. So, the sources of cash must equal the uses of cash on a sources/uses statement. Naturally, if we construct a sources/uses of cash statement and leave out an account, we will find that the sources/uses of cash statement does not balance. In this case, the gap between the sources and uses will indicate the cash effect of the missing account. If the sources of cash are greater than the uses of cash, it would indicate that the missing balance sheet account must have been a use of cash; i.e., cash flowed into that account. The gap between the sources and uses of cash is precisely how much cash the missing account used up. If the sources of cash are less than the uses of cash, however, this indicates that the missing account must have been a source of cash; that is, cash was generated by that account, and the magnitude of the cash generated is exactly equal to the difference between the sources and uses of cash.

For example, a cash flow accounting statement is simply a sources and uses of cash statement with the cash account missing. In this case, the gap between the sources and uses of cash indicates whether the cash account was a source of cash (whether the cash account decreased) or whether the cash account was a use of cash (whether the cash account increased).[7] For example, in ABC's cash flow statement (Figure 2.6), the category Other Assets and Liabilities used $24 million in 2013, as indicated by the –$24 million in the cash flow statement.

We can use this approach to develop a way to calculate free cash flow. Free cash flow is a measure of how much cash flows into the right-hand side of the balance sheet from the left-hand side. (Note here that when we refer to the right-hand side of the balance sheet, we are referring only to long-term liabilities such as debt and equity. All short-term liabilities such as accounts payable are placed on the left-hand side of the balance sheet as contra accounts. The net of short-term assets and the short-term liabilities in these contra accounts is net working capital account.) Specifically, we use a plug account to capture all the free cash flows into the right-hand side of the balance sheet; therefore, free cash flow is a measure of how much cash is flowing into this plug account.

So, if we simply leave out the plug account on the right-hand side of the balance sheet in a sources/uses of cash statement, the gap between the sources and uses of cash would tell us whether the missing accounts were a net source or a use of cash. In other words, with the plug account missing, the resulting gap between the sources and uses of cash would indicate whether cash flowed into the plug account or from the plug account as well as the magnitude of this cash flow.

Therefore, we can always calculate free cash flow by simply constructing a sources and uses of cash statement with the plug account excluded. If the resulting sources of cash are greater than the uses of cash, that scenario indicates that cash must then have flown to the right-hand side of the balance sheet from the left-hand side. Vice versa, if the resulting sources of cash are less than the uses of cash, that scenario indicates that cash flowed from the right-hand side of the balance sheet to the left-hand side. We now have a simple way of calculating free cash flow.

For example, let's refer back to Figure 2.5, the sources and uses of cash statement for ABC. However, let's create a new sources and uses of cash statement, placing the short-term liabilities in a separate section of the figure, treating them as contra-assets, as described earlier. The resulting representation is in Figure 4.3. The top portion is Assets, just as we showed earlier. However, we have now moved the short-term liabilities into a separate section—Contra-Assets—placed in the lower portion of the Assets section.

Figure 4.3 ABC Co.'s reorganized sources and uses of cash

ASSETS	Oct-13	Oct-12	Sources/(Uses) of Cash
Current assets:			
Cash and cash equivalents	670	911	241
Accounts receivable	1,519	1,540	21
Financing receivables	264	249	(15)
Inventory	624	539	(85)
Other current assets	1,175	1,277	102
Total current assets	4,252	4,515	264
Current Contra-Assets (from Liabilities side of the balance sheet)			
Notes payable and short-term borrowings	(674)	(587)	86
Accounts payable	(1,229)	(1,197)	32
Employee compensation and benefits	(333)	(355)	(21)
Taxes on earnings	(87)	(67)	21
Deferred revenue	(621)	(561)	60
Accrued restructuring	(55)	(76)	(21)
Other accrued liabilities	(1,205)	(1,275)	(70)
Total Current Contra-Assets	(4,204)	(4,117)	87
Net Working Capital	48	398	350

ASSETS	Oct-13	Oct-12	Sources/(Uses) of Cash
Other assets			
Property, plant and equipment	1,024	980	(44)
Long-term financing receivables and other assets	896	1,019	123
Other long term assets	6,975	5,477	(1,497)
Total Other Assets	8,895	7,476	(1,419)
Other Contra-Assets (from Liabilities side of the balance sheet)			
Other liabilities	(1,460)	(1,588)	(128)
Total Other Contra-Assets	(1,460)	(1,588)	(128)
Total assets	7,484	6,286	(1,197)
STOCKHOLDERS' EQUITY			
ABC stockholders' equity			
Preferred stock, $0.01 par value (300 shares authorized; none issued)			
Common stock, $0.01 par value (9,600 shares authorized; 1,991 and 2,204 shares issued and outstanding, respectively)	2	2	
Additional paid-in capital	1,150	1,150	
Retained earnings	4,453	3,863	
Total ABC stockholders' equity	5,604	5,015	
Total stockholders' equity	5,604	5,015	589
Change in Left-Hand Side of Balance Sheet + Change in Stockholders' Equity= "FREE CASH FLOW" (assuming no equity financing)			(608)
Long-term debt	1,879	1,272	608
Change in Right-Hand Side of the Balance sheet =			
Change in Long-Term Debt			**608**

* Positive sign represents "source" of cash. Negative sign represents "use" of cash.

Note: All figures are in millions of dollars.

To calculate free cash flow, we simply add up changes in cash generated by assets and changes in cash generated by contra-assets. This number is part of free cash flow. We also need to add in the change in stockholders' equity because the change in stockholders' equity is the result of net income, which is also a potential source of cash. As shown in Figure 4.3, for ABC the free cash flow generated between 2012 and 2013 was –$608 million. Notably, this is the same amount as the change in long-term debt (also shown in Figure 4.3). Essentially, the flow in cash occurred from the right-hand side of the balance sheet, in the form of an increase in long-term debt of $608 million. This flow offset the decline in cash generated by adding the change in the left-hand side of the balance sheet and the change in shareholders' equity.

With this approach, we can also see how changes in specific balance sheet accounts affect free cash flows. For example, suppose that we are running a manufacturing business and we consider a policy of increasing the amount of time we take to pay our suppliers. This would mean that our accounts payable would increase. The accounts payable is a short-term liability,[8] and you learned in Chapter 2 that an increase in a liability generates cash. Therefore, this policy of taking longer to pay suppliers would result in an increase in sources of cash and no changes to uses of cash. (We are assuming that this policy has no additional effects on the business, such as our suppliers charging us more as a penalty.) So, the net result is that additional cash is created on the left-hand side of the balance sheet and flows to the right-hand side of the balance sheet for distribution to debt and equity holders in the firm. So, if all else remains the same, a policy of taking longer to pay our vendors will result in increased free cash flow.

4.5 Free Cash Flow Calculation: A General Procedure

We now generalize the calculation of free cash flows. As discussed in the preceding section, a sources/uses of cash statement that reconciles to long-term debt essentially produces a measure of free cash flow. If we now simplify the balance sheet into a smaller set of macro accounts, we can develop a simple formula for free cash flows. Figure 4.4 shows such a balance sheet. The accounts on the left-hand side of the balance sheet have been grouped into two macro accounts: net working capital and long-term assets.

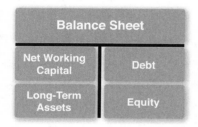

Figure 4.4 Balance sheet simplified into a smaller set of macro accounts

Net working capital consists of short-term assets (such as accounts receivable and inventory) minus short-term liabilities (such as accounts payable and deferred taxes). An important item to remember is that for all the calculations presented so far involving free cash flows, short-term liabilities have been moved to the left-hand side of the balance sheet. In effect, this creates a contra account on the left-hand side of the balance sheet for short-term liabilities. The sum of the short-term assets account and the short-term liabilities contra account equals net working capital. Another important thing to note is that the cash account, which is part of short-term assets, contains only cash needed to run the business (that is, operating cash). It does not contain excess cash. We discuss in a moment where to place excess cash.

With the identification of these two macro accounts, we can now state a general formula for calculating free cash flows. Because we are interested in cash generated by the left-hand side of the balance sheet and available to the right-hand side, we will generate a sources/uses of cash. Basically, free cash flow is given by the following formula:

$$FCF = -\, \Delta NWC - \Delta LTA \qquad\qquad (2)$$

NWC refers to net working capital, LTA refers to long-term assets, and Δ is a symbol denoting "change in." Therefore, this formula states that free cash flow can be computed by simply measuring the negative of the change in net working capital minus the change in long-term assets as we go forward in time. Because net working capital and long-term assets are asset-side accounts, an increase in these accounts uses cash (rather than generates cash) and will therefore decrease free cash flow.

There is one item missing from Equation 2. That is the cash generated from running the business. The cash account in net working capital contains only the cash needed to run the business. It does not contain the cash that was generated from running the business. So, we need to include this into our free cash flow calculation. The following modified equation for free cash flow includes this cash generated by the business:

$$FCF = EBIAT - \Delta NWC - \Delta LTA \qquad\qquad (3)$$

EBIAT refers to *earnings before interest and after taxes*. EBIAT is basically after-tax operating profits. One might wonder why we are using EBIAT rather than the traditional net income account to measure cash generated by the business. In fact, EBIAT and net income are quite close. The primary difference between the two is that net income includes interest paid on debt as an expense (along with the associated tax shield), whereas EBIAT is before interest so that it does not include any interest expense. To measure free cash flow, we want to exclude the right-hand side of the balance sheet, including any effects of capital structure decisions (decisions about the debt versus equity composition of the financing of the firm). Interest expense is a direct effect of capital structure policy. The more debt a firm uses, the higher its interest expense, and vice versa. Because we are only interested in cash generated from running the business (that is, the left-hand side of the balance sheet), we do not want to include interest expense in our measure of free cash flow. Therefore, we use EBIAT rather than net income. As a result, the free cash flow measure in Equation 3 is a measure of all cash that is generated by the left-hand side of the balance sheet and available for distribution to the financial claimants on the right-hand side of the balance sheet (in the form of interest, principal repayments, dividends, stock buybacks, and so on).

Because new working capital only contains cash needed to run the business, EBIAT fills in the missing piece in the free cash flow formula for cash thrown off from operating the business. Equation 3 states that free cash flow is simply equal to minus the changes (increases) in net working capital and long-term assets as a result of running the basic business and the cash generated from running this business.

We will make one more change to the free cash flow formula by defining long-term assets more clearly. Long-term assets are simply the long-term fixed assets, or net property, plant, and equipment (PPE) of the business. The net PPE account can be broken down into two accounts: gross PPE and accumulated depreciation. Gross PPE is simply the total amount spent on long-term fixed assets since the inception of the firm. The gross PPE account includes expenditures for both acquisition of new PPE and maintenance of existing PPE. Accumulated depreciation is an account that captures the total depreciation since the inception of the firm. Every time a depreciation expense is taken, that amount is added to the accumulated depreciation account. The net of gross PPE and accumulated depreciation is net PPE, which is effectively the firm's current PPE level. The following equation summarizes our breakdown of the net PPE account:

$$LTA = Net\ PPE = Gross\ PPE - Accum\ Depr \qquad (4)$$

We are using Accum Depr to denote accumulated depreciation. If long-term assets equals gross PPE minus accumulated depreciation, the change in long-term assets must be equal to the change in gross PPE minus the change in accumulated depreciation:

$$\Delta LTA = \Delta Net\ PPE = \Delta Gross\ PPE - \Delta Accum\ Depr \qquad (5)$$

Of course, the change in gross PPE in a given period is simply equal to the capital expenditure for that period. Similarly, the change in accumulated depreciation is simply equal to the depreciation expense for that period. Therefore, we have

$$\Delta LTA = \Delta Net\ PPE = CapEx - Depr \qquad (6)$$

where CapEx denotes capital expenditure, and Depr denotes depreciation. We can now substitute this result into Equation 3:

$$FCF = EBIAT - \Delta NWC - CapEx + Depr \qquad (7)$$

This is our final free cash flow formula, and we will use it for the remainder of this book. This formula basically says that free cash flow during a specific period equals the cash generated by the business during that period minus any changes (increase) in net working capital during the period minus any capital expenditures during the period plus the depreciation expense taken during the period. This free cash flow is then available for distribution to all financial claimants on the right-hand side of the balance sheet.

The following example using the forecasted financial statements from Chapter 3 for ABC Co. illustrates how to use the free cash formula in Equation 7 to calculate free cash flows for a company. In Figure 4.5, we implement the free cash flow formula to forecast free cash flows for ABC from 2014 through 2018. In 2014, for example, our first step is to calculate earnings before interest and taxes (EBIT), which is simply total net revenue minus cost of goods sold (COGS) (which includes the cost of products, cost of services, and financing interest), research and development expenses (R&D), SG&A expenses, and other expenses. This produces an EBIT value of $887M for 2014.

We then subtract taxes from this to produce the EBIAT value needed in the free cash flow formula. The tax rate used is the same as the tax rate projected in Figure 3.1, which is 21.24%. This calculation produces an EBIAT value of $699M for 2014. We then subtract out the changes in net working capital. Net working capital is computed for each year: $53M in 2014 and $48M in 2013 (not shown in Figure 4.5). Therefore, net working capital increased by $5M in 2014.

Figure 4.5 Financial Projections ($MM)

	2014	2015	2016	2017	2018
Net Revenue	11,664	12,831	14,114	15,525	17,077
COGS	8,940	9,834	10,818	11,899	13,089
R&D	298	328	361	397	437
SG&A	1,234	1,358	1,494	1,643	1,807
Other Expenses	304	335	368	405	445
EBIT	887	976	1,073	1,181	1,299
Taxes	188	207	228	251	276
EBIAT	699	768	845	930	1,023
NWC	53	58	64	71	78
Change in NWC	5	5	6	6	7
PP&E (Beginning of Year)	8,895	9,785	10,763	11,840	13,024
Capital Expenditures	1,383	1,522	1,674	1,841	2,025
Depreciation	494	543	597	657	723
PP&E (End of Year)	9,785	10,763	11,840	13,024	14,326
Free Cash Flow	−196	−215	−237	−261	−287

To finish calculating free cash flow for 2014, we need to determine capital expenditures and depreciation. The first thing we do to determine this is to determine property, plant, and equipment (PP&E) levels at the beginning of year (BoY) and at the end of year (EoY). In calculating PP&E, we will include the accounts Property,

Plant, and Equipment, as well as long-term financing receivables, and other long-term assets. The beginning of year value for 2014 is simply the EoY value for 2013. This is $8,895M. The EoY value for 2014 is $9,785M. We can now determine capital expenditures and depreciation using the following equation, which has to hold each year:

$$PP\&E\ (BoY) + CapEx - Depr = PP\&E\ (EoY) \qquad (8)$$

This equation simply states that ending PP&E balance each year must be equal to the starting PP&E balance for that year plus any capital expenditures that were made that year (as these would add to the PP&E that a firm owns) minus any depreciation for that year (as these would reduce the value of PP&E that a firm owns). For 2014, we know two of the items in this equation already: PP&E (BoY) and PP&E (EoY). So, if we can determine one of the remaining quantities, the other one will be automatically determined by Equation 8. We will determine the depreciation amount for 2014 by maintaining the previous year's depreciation level as a percentage of beginning of year PP&E. This turns out to be $415 / (980 + 1,019 + 5,477) = 5.55\%$ for 2013. So, if we maintain this percentage for 2014, the forecasted depreciation expense will be 5.55% times beginning of year PP&E ($1,024 + 896 + 6,975 = 8,895$). This yields a 2014 depreciation amount of $5.55\% \times 8895 = 494$. Then, from Equation 8, the capital expenditures can be determined as $9785 + 494 - 8,895 = 1,383$. Thus, we now have determined all the components needed to calculate the free cash flow formula. For 2014, this turns out to be –$196M. As a result, our plug accounts, long-term debt, and other long-term liabilities[9] must increase by $196M in 2014 to produce the needed cash for the left-hand side of the balance sheet.

The free cash flow calculations for the years from 2015 through 2018 in Figure 4.5 follow a similar approach. We will use the cash flows in this example in later chapters as we develop our overall valuation framework.

We will develop another example to demonstrate how to value a project. Let's analyze the following project in which ABC Co. is considering investing. The project is a new product introduction. The new product will require an initial investment of $20M per year for two years to develop a new manufacturing facility. This facility would be depreciated straight-line to a zero salvage value over five years. After the manufacturing plant is built, sales would begin (in Year 3 of the project). However, in preparation for new sales, an investment would need to be made during the second year to build up a parts inventory and cash needed for short-term needs. This investment would be equal to 25% of expected sales in the following year, and this investment would need to remain in place at 25% of expected next-year sales throughout the life of the product. The new product is expected to generate sales of $71.4M in the first year that it is introduced, $82.8M in its second year, $43.4M in its third and fourth years, and $21.6M in its fifth and final year, after which the product would be dropped as it would become obsolete. The gross margins for the product (which include the depreciation expense) are expected to be 29% each year there are sales. Other costs for running this new business would be 10% of sales. The marginal tax rate for the ABC is 25%.

Figure 4.6 contains the free cash flows for this project. For the first two years, we are investing $20M each year to build a manufacturing plant. These investments get captured as capital expenditures (CapEx). Once the plant is built, the total $40M investment is depreciated over a five-year period ($8M per year), which results in a depreciation expense of $8M per year. Because there are no sales or investment in net working capital in 2014, applying Equation 7 gives a free cash flow (FCF) of –$20M for 2014. Because sales are expected to be $71.4M in the first year, net working capital of $71.4M × 25% = $17.85M must be in place.[10] Therefore, the NWC balance at the end of 2015 (beginning of 2016) is $17.85M. Thus, there is an increase in NWC in 2015 of $17.85M (as NWC was zero in the prior year).

So, applying Equation 7 gives a total free cash flow of –$37.85M for 2015. The first year of sales is 2016. Sales are $71.4M. Due to the 29% gross margin, the cost of goods sold (COGS) is $71.4M × (1 – 29%) = $50.69M. Selling, general, and administrative (SG&A) expenses are 10% of sales: $71.4M × 10% = $7.14M. Therefore EBIT for 2016 is $13.57M, and EBIAT at a 25% tax rate is $10.18M. There is no further CapEx because the plant is now fully built; however, the plant begins depreciating and so there is a depreciation expense of $8M. Applying Equation 7 gives a free cash flow amount of $15.33M for 2016. The calculations for future years follow in a similar manner. The question of whether to undertake this project requires us to determine how much value is created (or destroyed) if ABC Co. undertakes the project. We will continue this example and do this valuation in Chapter 6, "Putting It All Together: Valuation Frameworks."

Figure 4.6 Financial Projections ($000s)

	2014	2015	2016	2017	2018	2019	2020
Sales			71,400	82,800	82,800	43,400	21,600
COGS			50,694	58,788	58,788	30,814	15,336
SG&A			7,140	8,280	8,280	4,340	2,160
EBIT			13,566	15,732	15,732	8,246	4,104
EBIAT			10,175	11,799	11,799	6,185	3,078
NWC		17,850	20,700	20,700	10,850	5,400	0
Change in NWC		17,850	2,850	0	–9,850		–5,400
CapEx	20,000	20,000					
Depr			8,000	8,000	8,000	8,000	8,000
FCF	–20,000	–37,850	15,325	19,799	29,649	14,185	16,478

4.6 Free Cash Flow Calculation: Another View

We developed the free cash formula in Equation 7 by looking at whether different balance sheet accounts are sources or uses of cash, but there is another way to view this free cash flow formula. Although it is quite similar to the approach we used in the previous section, it provides additional intuition about why the free cash formula works as it does. This section introduces this alternative approach.

If we want to calculate free cash flow, rather than starting with the balance sheet as we did in the previous section, we could instead start with the income statement. In other words, to calculate free cash flow, we start with the business and how much cash the operations throw off. This, of course, is given by net income. However, we need to recognize just as we did before that free cash flow is really about how much cash is generated by the business independent of capital structure decisions. So, we want to exclude interest expense. This leads us to EBIAT, just as in the previous section.

Another item to note about net income is that there may be noncash expenses in the income statement. The most common one is depreciation, so we will represent all noncash charges with this term. Because depreciation is really a noncash charge, it really should not affect free cash flow. However, because depreciation is not excluded from the income statement, we need take it out and create a new operating cash flow result called *EBIDAT* (earnings before interest, depreciation, and after taxes). This could be our starting point for calculating free cash flows. However, this leaves another minor problem. Even though depreciation is a noncash charge and should not be included in free cash flows, it does provide the company a tax shield, which is an actual cash saving. The IRS allows firms to deduct depreciation as an expense in the calculation of their taxes. This depreciation expense thus lowers the company's tax bill, which is a real cash saving for the firm. Therefore, we cannot fully take out the depreciation expense in EBIDAT. A portion of it (the tax savings) needs to remain in the free cash flow formula. This is solved in the following common way. We start the free cash flow calculation with EBIAT, just as we did before. Because EBIAT contains depreciation as an expense, it contains the depreciation tax shield.

However, because the depreciation expense itself should not be included in the free cash flow calculation, we add back the depreciation as a separate step. We therefore have the result

$$Cash\ Flow\ from\ Operations = EBIAT + Depr \qquad (9)$$

To calculate free cash flow, we now just need to include the effect of operations on the asset side accounts, which are net working capital and net PPE. Specifically, we want the cash effects to these two accounts. Therefore, we want to subtract out any increase in net working capital, and we want to subtract any capital expenditures. This leads to the same result that we calculated in the previous section:

$$FCF = Cash\ Flow\ from\ Operations - \Delta NWC - CapEx \quad (10)$$

$$= EBIAT + Depr - \Delta NWC - CapEx \qquad (11)$$

This provides another perspective on the formula for calculating free cash flows, which is more income statement centric rather than the balance sheet centric approach used in the previous section. Both approaches are quite similar, and both of course lead to the same final free cash flow formula.

Endnotes

1 Recall that the plug account may be placed anywhere in the balance sheet. Different locations in the balance sheet will result in different interpretations of what form of financing the plug account denotes.

2 The final part of this process is to then make sure that this amount and form of financing are in place (i.e., to execute the amount and form of financing). We talk more about this later in the book.

3 Note that this is not the same as the accounting definition of cash flow that we discussed in Chapter 2. The accounting definition of free cash flow, for example, incorporates the effects of financing into its definition of cash flow. Free cash flow, however, does not incorporate financing effects because it is largely driven by the left-hand side of the balance sheet. For this reason, free cash flow is sometimes referred to as operating cash flow to clearly distinguish it from the accounting definition of cash flow.

4 As mentioned previously, this view changes for financial institutions. In a financial institution, both the left-hand and right-hand sides of the balance sheet contain the operating activities.

5 It is important to note that by debt, we specifically refer to long-term debt. Short-term liabilities such as accounts payable or notes payable that typically are categorized as part of working capital are moved to the left-hand side of the balance sheet. On the left-hand side, they show up as contra accounts and are netted against short-term assets such as inventory and accounts receivable. We then net these short-term assets and the contra accounts representing the short-term liabilities to form an asset-side account called net working capital. So whenever we refer to a balance sheet as having net working capital, it automatically indicates that the liability-side of the balance sheet only contains long-term liabilities.

6 As discussed in Chapter 3, future operating activity targets automatically imply a certain set of balances in all the accounts on the left-hand side of the balance sheet.

7 This is why accountants usually refer to a cash flow statement as reconciling to the cash account.

8 Again, note that even though this item is a liability, we are considering it a left-hand side account; i.e., it is a contra asset account.

9 Note that we are using a slightly different interpretation of other long-term liabilities here than was used earlier in Figure 4.3 with regard to the sources and uses of cash. Here, we are treating other long-term liabilities as a potential financing vehicle (like long-term debt), whereas we had treated this as a contra-long-term asset account earlier. An example of a long-term financing vehicle might be hybrid securities such as convertible notes.

10 As sales increase, the working capital will need to increase, and there will be further investments into working capital, which in turn will create negative cash flow. However, as sales decrease in later years, the working capital amount can be reduced, thus creating positive cash flow as the firm takes back working capital from the project.

5

Cost of Capital

5.1 Introduction

As stated in Chapter 1, "Introduction," the primary goal of this book is to develop the methodology for measuring the value of any business decision, ranging from decisions such as going forward with a project (such as a new product introduction) or to acquisition decisions (such as purchasing another business). To do this, we need to evaluate the following present value relation:

$$Value_0 = \frac{E(CF_1)}{1+r} + \frac{E(CF_2)}{(1+r)^2} + \frac{E(CF_3)}{(1+r)^3} + \dots \tag{1}$$

where $E(CF_1)$, $E(CF_2)$, and so on are expected future cash flows, r denotes a discount rate, and $Value_0$ is the value of the project that we are trying to measure. Chapter 4, "Free Cash Flows," discussed how the numerators in this formula are computed. Each year we construct projected financial statements for the project that we are interested in valuing, and we then calculate free cash flows from these financials. The free cash flows are the numbers that are used in the numerator in the present value equation.

There is now only one piece missing: the denominators. This chapter shows how to compute the denominators in Equation 1. The basic idea is that the denominators represent discount rates, or expected rates of return. In general, rates of return correspond to risk. The higher the risk, the higher the rate of return. The rate of return in the denominator of any particular term in Equation 1 corresponds to the risk of the free cash flow in the numerator of that term. Hence to determine the discount rates needed for Equation 1, we will have to define risk and develop a relationship between risk and return. Then, all we have to do is to measure the risk of each projected free cash flow for the specific project we are evaluating, and we will use this risk-return relationship to determine the corresponding return, which we can plug into the denominator of the term in Equation 1 containing that free cash flow.

5.2 Risk and Return

If one were to invest in a zero-coupon, one-year U.S. Treasury bill that cost $95 and paid $100 in one year, the expected return on this security would be

$$\frac{\$100}{\$95} - 1 = 5.26\%$$

Of course, because this is a risk-free security,[1] the expected return of 5.26% will also be the realized return on the security. However, all securities, with a very few exceptions such as U.S. Treasuries, contain risk. What this means is that a typical security contains risk for the investor. Suppose, for instance, that the one-year bond previously described was issued by a corporation rather than the U.S. Treasury. Suppose also that this company has a 10% chance of defaulting in the next year, and if the company defaults, the bondholder will receive only $95. Due to the uncertainty of whether the company will default in the coming year, suppose that investors are now willing to pay only $93 for this security. The expected return of this security is now

$$(\frac{\$100}{\$93} \times 90\% + \frac{\$95}{\$93} \times 10\%) - 1 = 6.99\%$$

Notice that the expected return for the corporate bond is higher than the Treasury bond. This is because of the uncertainty due to default. Investors are asking for a higher expected return because they are bearing greater uncertainty, or risk, about the possible pay-out of the bond one year from now. Investors get this higher expected return by paying a lower price for the bond today. The difference in expected return between the risky corporate bond risk-free Treasury bill is called a *risk premium.* In the preceding example, the risk premium paid by the corporate bond to investors is 6.99% − 5.26% = 1.73%.[2] The risk premium for a Treasury security is 0% (because there is no possibility of default). This reveals an important concept about risk and risk premium. As risk increases, so does the risk premium; i.e., as investors bear more risk, they command a higher risk premium. This is perhaps the most fundamental principle of finance.[3]

For the purposes of evaluating Equation 1, we need to be able to calculate the expected return of all assets (including traded securities, like the corporate bond above). The difficulty is that for nearly all risky assets, including corporate bonds, it is difficult to evaluate the amount of risk in that asset. In the previous example, we stated that the risk of a default by the company is 10% and that investors would receive $95 at maturity in the case of a default. In reality, these are statements about the future, and therefore we would have a very difficult time quantifying exactly what the probability of default is and what the payoff in the case of default would be.[4] So, we have to figure out a way to calculate the risk and expected returns for assets without knowing precisely all the potential future scenarios and payoffs in those scenarios.

The first step is to develop a way to measure risk. What makes a security risky is uncertainty to the investor about the payoff resulting from holding that security. In the preceding example, we assumed that the investor would hold the corporate bond to maturity, and the bond would pay either $100 or $95. The uncertainty of whether he receives $100 or $95 is defined as risk. However, the investor may decide to sell the security to a second investor before maturity. In this case, how much would the first investor receive for the sale? This is unknown. Many things may change in the economy, the company, the markets, and so on between now and the time of the sale. All of these changes would likely cause the second investor to attach a different probability of bankruptcy and different payoff if bankruptcy occurs to the corporate bond, which would result in a different price for the bond. This, too, represents risk to the first investor. The payoff to this investor from holding this bond is the sale price to the second investor, but this sale price is unknown, and therefore risky. So, the possibility of movement at any time in the price of assets one is holding represents the true risk of that asset. These price movements will generate varying returns to the investor in that asset. Therefore, rather than using prices, we can re-express risk in terms of returns: the possibility of generating variable returns from holding an asset represents the risk of that asset.

How do we measure the degree of variability in the returns that an asset produces? We use the simple statistical concept of standard deviation. Suppose that we have a stock and we are interested in measuring its risk. Suppose that in each of the past four months, the stock has produced the following returns: 4%, –3%, 5%, 2%. The risk of the stock is measured by the variability of the stock's returns that an investor would face. We will measure this variability by calculating the standard deviation of the stock's returns over the past four months. First, the mean return for the stock over the past four months is

$$\mu = \frac{4\% - 3\% + 5\% + 2\%}{4}$$
$$= 2\% \text{ per month}$$

We use μ to denote the stock's mean return. Normally, we quote mean returns on an annualized basis. Therefore, the stock has an average return of 24% per annum.[5] We can now calculate the standard deviation of the stock:

$$\sigma^2 = \frac{(4\% - 2\%)^2 + (-3\% - 2\%)^2 + (5\% - 2\%)^2 + (2\% - 2\%)^2}{4}$$

$$= 0.095\%$$

We use σ^2 to denote variance. The standard deviation, σ, is therefore

$$\sigma = \sqrt{\frac{(4\% - 2\%)^2 + (-3\% - 2\%)^2 + (5\% - 2\%)^2 + (2\% - 2\%)^2}{4}}$$

$$= 3.08\%$$

Just as with average return, we typically quote standard deviation, or volatility, on an annualized basis. The annualized volatility of the stock is therefore $3.08\% \times \sqrt{12} = 10.7\%$. We now have a way of measuring the risk of a stock.

We will present one more investment concept, which we will need in subsequent sections. To gauge the value of a stock, it is not enough to know just the risk. The risk is simply the cost that investors have to pay (or bear) to gain the benefits from holding the stock. The benefit is the expected return. To do cost-benefit analysis of stocks and other assets, we would like to have a single metric that captures both the cost and the benefit of holding an asset. Many such metrics exist, but the simplest one is the *Sharpe* ratio:

$$S_A = \frac{\mu_A - R_f}{\sigma_A} \qquad (2)$$

For any asset A, the Sharpe ratio, S_A, of that asset is defined as that asset's expected return, μ_A, minus the risk-free rate, R_f, divided by the asset's volatility, σ_A. The numerator of this equation is the asset's risk premium, and the denominator is the risk of the asset. Therefore, the Sharpe ratio for any asset gives us that asset's benefit per unit of risk for the investor that owns the asset. Obviously, higher Sharpe ratios are always more desirable for investors.

In the example above for the stock, if the risk-free rate is 4% per annum, and the stock's mean return of 24% also represents its expected return, the Sharpe ratio of the stock is given by

$$S = \frac{24\% - 4\%}{10.7\%}$$
$$= 1.87$$

Figure 5.1 presents a graphical way of thinking about the Sharpe ratio. This figure contains a risk-return graph. The horizontal axis represents the level of risk, and the vertical axis represents the level of expected return. Any asset in the investment universe can be placed as a point in this graph depending on its risk and expected return. The graph shows as an example of a stock with a volatility level of 10% and an expected return of 12%. There is also a risk-free asset with a volatility of 0% and an expected return of 2.5%. The Sharpe ratio of this stock is simply the slope of the line passing through both the risk-free asset and the stock. In general, the Sharpe ratio of any asset is the slope of the line passing through both that asset and the risk-free asset.

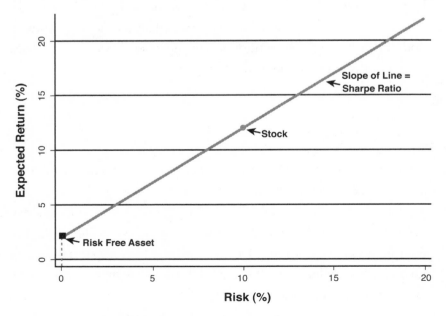

Figure 5.1 Graphical representation of the Sharpe ratio

5.3 Risk Reduction through Diversification

An important question that we need to answer is what happens to the risk an investor bears when he owns more than one type of asset. In addition, a more important question is what happens to the Sharpe ratio of the investor's portfolio when he holds more than one type of asset. This section answers these questions, which will then set up the next two sections concerning how to generate a discount rate, or required rate of return, for any asset.

Because we are using the statistical property of standard deviation to measure an asset's risk, we can simply extend this approach to calculate risk when there is more than one asset. Suppose we have two assets, A and B, in a portfolio. Asset A has an expected return of μ_A and a volatility of σ_A. Meanwhile, asset B has an expected return of μ_B and a volatility of σ_B. What is the expected return and volatility of an investor's portfolio if he holds both A and B? To answer this, we need two more pieces of information. First, we need to know how much the investor has invested into each of A and B (i.e., what fraction of the portfolio contains A and what fraction contains B). Suppose that w_A represents the fraction of the investor's portfolio invested in asset A, and w_B represents the fraction invested in B.[6] The second piece of information that we need is the relationship between the price movements of A and B; e.g., when A moves up 1%, what is B likely to do? We will use the statistical property of correlation to describe this relationship. We assume that A's returns and B's returns have a correlation of ρ. We can now state the expected return and volatility of the portfolio. The expected return of the portfolio is given by

$$\mu_P = w_A \mu_A + w_B \mu_B \tag{3}$$

where μ_P denotes the expected return of the portfolio. The volatility of the portfolio is given by

$$\sigma_P = \sqrt{w_A^2 \sigma_A^2 + w_B^2 \sigma_B^2 + 2\rho w_A w_B \sigma_A \sigma_B} \tag{4}$$

where σ_P denotes the portfolio's volatility.

It is easiest to understand these formulas through an example. Suppose that we start with the stock in the example in the previous section. This stock had an expected return of 24.0% and a volatility of 10.7%. As we calculated earlier, the Sharpe ratio of this stock is 1.87, assuming a risk-free rate of 4%. Suppose that we also have a second stock with an expected return of 15% and a volatility of 12%. The Sharpe ratio for this stock is (15% – 4%) / 12% = 0.92. Assume that the correlation between the two stocks is 0.1.

Initially, it might not appear to make any sense to invest in stock 2. After all, why should one invest any money in a stock with a Sharpe ratio of 0.92 when one could instead invest in a stock with a much higher Sharpe ratio of 1.87. Putting some of the portfolio into the lower Sharpe ratio stock would seemingly only lower the Sharpe ratio of the portfolio down from 1.87.

Let's check this intuition by putting 70% of the portfolio into stock 1 (the higher Sharpe ratio stock) and 30% of the portfolio into stock 2. Plugging these values into Equations 3 and 4, we can calculate that the portfolio has an expected return of 21.3% and a volatility of 8.6%. This means that the portfolio has a Sharpe ratio of 2.0. Contrary to what our intuition may have suggested, the Sharpe ratio of the portfolio went up rather than decreasing below the Sharpe ratio of stock 1 alone.

The key to the increase in Sharpe ratio is the fact that the volatility of the portfolio of the two stocks actually decreased below the volatility of each of the individual stocks. This occurs because of the low correlation between the two stocks. This low correlation means that when one stock goes up, the other has a good chance of going down. And vice versa, when one stock goes down, the other has a good chance of going up. Therefore, due to the low correlation, one stock always has a good chance of counteracting the movement of the other stock.

This offsetting of individual stock price movements means that the movement of the portfolio as a whole decreases. The result is a lower volatility for the portfolio of the two stocks than for either stock individually. We call this effect *diversification*. Due to diversification, the volatility of the portfolio drops substantially. Meanwhile the expected return is simply a weighed average of the two individual stocks. As a result, the Sharpe ratio of the portfolio increases.

Figure 5.2 uses the risk-return graph presented in the previous section to demonstrate what happens as we move from a portfolio that is 100% invested in stock 1 to a portfolio that has a mix of stock 1 and stock 2 to a portfolio that is 100% invested in stock 2. The curved line represents the risk-return point of the portfolio as it moves gradually from a 100% investment in stock 1 to a 100% investment in stock 2. The slopes of the straight lines represent Sharpe ratios of the portfolio when it 100% invested in stock 1, when it contains a mix of stock 1 and stock 2, and when it is 100% invested in stock 2. Due to the diversification effect, the Sharpe ratio starts increasing as we start with the 100% stock 1 portfolio and add more and more of stock 2. At some point, however, the portfolio begins to contain mostly stock 2, and the Sharpe ratio starts decreasing. Notice that there is a mix of stock 1 and stock 2, which maximizes the Sharpe ratio. At this point (as well as neighboring points), the Sharpe ratio of the portfolio is higher than the Sharpe ratio of either stock 1 alone or stock 2 alone.

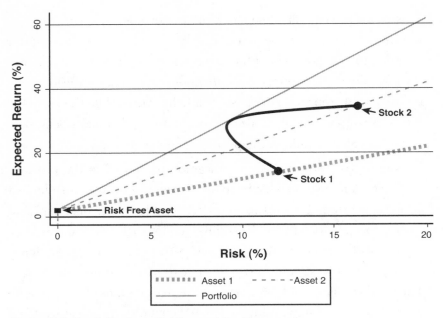

Figure 5.2 Portfolio diversification and the Sharpe ratio

The principle of diversification is one of the most important principles of investing. It says that achieving a high Sharpe ratio is not just about investing in stocks that have high expected return and low volatility (i.e., high Sharpe ratios). It is also about investing in stocks that have low correlations with other stocks. Due to the effects of diversification, these low-correlation stocks will drive the volatility of the portfolio substantially lower, thus increasing the portfolio's Sharpe ratio above what one could achieve with an investment in high Sharpe ratio stocks alone.

5.4 Systematic Versus Unsystematic Risk

Due to the principle of diversification, if we place two uncorrelated (with correlation less than one) assets in a portfolio, the risk of the portfolio can be lower than that of either individual asset. Furthermore, the Sharpe ratio of the portfolio will be higher than the Sharpe ratio of either individual asset. This is because the less-than-perfect correlation between the two assets means that some of the variation of one asset will be counteracted by some of the variation of the second asset, thereby dampening the volatility of the portfolio.

We can carry the diversification principle further. Suppose that we take this portfolio of two assets and we add another asset to it. The same principle applies. We can reduce the volatility of the portfolio and increase its Sharpe ratio. Now, we can repeat this again. We can add a fourth asset to the portfolio and reduce its volatility and increase its Sharpe ratio. In fact, we can keep adding assets to the portfolio, and as long as the assets being added are less than perfectly correlated with the portfolio, the addition will lower the volatility of the portfolio a bit more and increase its Sharpe ratio a bit more.

So, how far can we lower the volatility of the portfolio? Figures 5.3 and 5.4 shows what happens as we keep adding assets to the portfolio. As we add more and more assets, the volatility of the portfolio converges to a lower bound, and the Sharpe ratio of the portfolio converges to an upper bound. The lower bound and upper bound are achieved essentially when every asset in the investable universe has been added to the portfolio. This portfolio, therefore, is called the *world market portfolio,* and the volatility of the market portfolio (the lower volatility bound) is known as market volatility, or *market risk.*

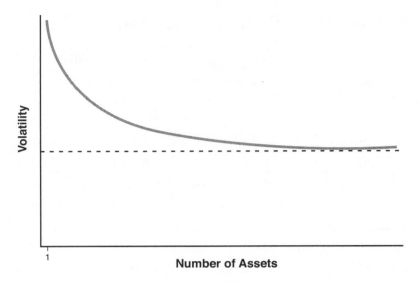

Figure 5.3 Portfolio diversification and volatility

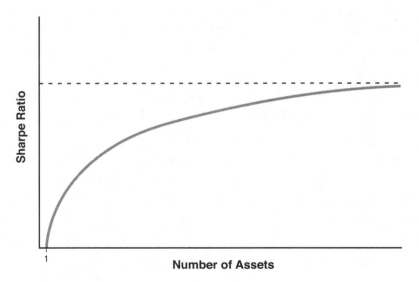

Figure 5.4 Portfolio diversification and the Sharpe ratio

Another name for market risk is *nondiversifiable risk*. For any individual asset in the world market portfolio, the bulk of its risk is diversified away by all the other assets in the portfolio. As we add more and more assets to the world market portfolio, the total risk of any individual asset decreases until it contains only its contribution to market risk. Because there are quite a lot of investable assets in the world, an individual security's remaining risk after diversification (its market risk contribution) is nearly the same as market risk. Therefore, we tend to think of the total risk of any individual security as composed of two pieces: a diversifiable component (i.e., diversifiable risk) and a market component (i.e., nondiversifiable risk).

Total Risk = Diversifiable Risk + Nondiversifiable Risk   (5)

= Diversifiable Risk + Market-Related Risk   (6)

Market-related risk cannot be diversified away by an investor no matter how much he diversifies his portfolio. It is risk that is inherent to the global economic system. Therefore, investors also refer to this form of risk as *systematic risk* (and to diversifiable risk as *nonsystematic risk*). Examples of risk inherent to the global economic system would be the risk of a world war, an international trade dispute, an increase in the yield curve, and the introduction of new computer technology. Examples of nonsystematic risk include the risk of an individual firm's CEO dying, the sudden departure of an individual firm's star salesperson, and a union strike at an individual manufacturing plant. Notice that in the examples of nonsystematic risk, the risks are typically specific to an individual firm. That is because these risks are completely uncorrelated to the global economic system and therefore are easily diversified away. For this reason, other names for diversifiable risk include *firm-specific risk* and *idiosyncratic risk*.

5.5 The Capital Asset Pricing Model

Just as the volatility of the world market portfolio is a lower bound, the Sharpe ratio of the world market portfolio is an upper bound and is known as the market Sharpe ratio. The market Sharpe ratio plays a special role in the determination of the cost of capital for any invest-able asset.

As discussed in the preceding section, when we add an asset to the world market portfolio, that asset's diversifiable, or nonsystematic, risk gets diversified away. This leaves only the systematic risk of that asset. Therefore, when an investor invests in an asset, if he holds only that asset, then he bears total risk, both nonsystematic and systematic risk. However, if the investor holds the market portfolio and invests in that asset and adds it to his market portfolio, then he bears only systematic risk. We discussed earlier that as an investor bears more risk, he needs to be paid a higher rate of return, or risk premium, to compensate him for that higher risk. So, then the question naturally arises as to which is the relevant risk—systematic, nonsystematic, or total risk—for which he should earn a risk premium.

If we think of a risk premium as a reward for bearing risk, then we should only reward an investor for bearing risk that needs to be borne (i.e., that some investor in the world needs to bear because it cannot be eliminated). The answer then is very simple. The relevant risk of any asset is its systematic risk. The nonsystematic risk in any asset can be easily eliminated by any investor by simply diversifying his portfolio. Therefore, both nonsystematic risk and the nonsystematic component of total risk can be eliminated. Systematic risk cannot be eliminated; it must be borne by somebody. Therefore, the market rewards an investor who is willing to bear the systematic risk in an asset by paying a risk premium. How much of a risk premium does the market pay for holding an asset?

The risk premium for any security should be tied to the amount of systematic risk in that asset. Let's start with the easiest asset: the world market portfolio. The world market portfolio only contains systematic risk (because all nonsystematic risk has been diversified away). Suppose we define the market Sharpe ratio (the Sharpe ratio of the world market portfolio) as S_M. So, we can conclude that for pure systematic risk, an investor earns a risk premium per unit of systematic risk (recall that this is the definition of a Sharpe ratio) equal to S_M. Now let's consider the case of an asset that is not the world market portfolio. The market pays a risk premium for only the systematic risk in that asset. How do we measure the systematic risk in an asset? We can simply measure the correlation of that asset to the world market portfolio. If the correlation is one, then the asset contains only systematic risk and its Sharpe ratio should be the same as that of the world market portfolio. If its correlation is zero, then it contains no systematic risk, and its Sharpe ratio should be zero; i.e., the market should not pay any risk premium to an investor for holding this asset because the asset contains only nonsystematic risk. If the correlation is something other than one or zero, suppose it is ρ_A, the Sharpe ratio of the asset, S_A is given by

$$SA = \rho ASM \tag{7}$$

This equation just states that the Sharpe ratio of any asset is equal to the correlation of that asset with the world market portfolio times the Sharpe ratio of the world market portfolio, S_M. Notice that if the correlation is zero or one, we get precisely the Sharpe ratio that we described earlier.

We will now expand this equation by explicitly writing out the Sharpe ratio as the ratio of the risk premium of an asset and its volatility:

$$\frac{R_A - R_f}{\sigma_A} = \rho_A \frac{R_M - R_f}{\sigma_M} \tag{8}$$

where R_A and σ_A denote the asset's expected return and volatility, R_M and σ_M denote the world market portfolio's expected return and volatility, ρ denotes the correlation between the asset and the world market portfolio, and R_f denotes the risk-free rate. We can rearrange this equation to obtain the risk premium for the asset:

$$R_A - R_f = \frac{\rho_A \sigma_A}{\sigma_M}(R_M - R_f)$$

$$(9)$$

For simplicity, we will denote the term $\frac{\rho_A \sigma_A}{\sigma_M}$ as simply as β_A.

$$R_A - R_f = \beta_A(R_M - R_f)$$

$$(10)$$

This equation is known as the *capital asset pricing model* (CAPM), and it enables us to calculate the risk premium of any asset. The term β_A is known as the beta of an asset, and it is a measure of the systematic risk in an asset. Therefore, the higher the beta, the higher the risk premium the market pays for an asset. Examples of low beta assets would be the stock of a utility or a food company. Regardless of what happens in the global economic system, consumers are unlikely to change the consumption of gas, electricity, or food by very much. Therefore, these stocks would have low correlations with the world market portfolio, which would result in a low betas (typically around 0.6 or 0.7). Conversely, the stock of a business equipment manufacturer or a steel producer would tend to have a high beta. If a downturn in the global economy occurs, businesses tend to cut back on production, and there is less office construction, which in turn leads to lower demand for business equipment and steel, respectively. By the same argument, in a global economic upturn, demand for these products would be high. Therefore, these stocks tend to be highly correlated with the world market portfolio. As a result, their betas tend to be high (typically around 1.2 or 1.3).

As an example, let's calculate the risk premium for the stock of a food manufacturer with a beta of 0.7. With the β known, the only thing that we have to calculate is $R_M - R_f$, the world market risk premium. Of course, we would like to calculate the expected risk premium for the world market going forward. However, we have no way of looking into the future. Instead, we will do the best we can by utilizing historical data on the world market risk premium. We need to collect data on all of the world's markets, which presents a major challenge. Data on the U.S. markets exist for over a hundred years, but most asset markets in the world have existed (or we only have satisfactory data on them) for only one or two decades at best. Because we are going to use historical data to estimate an expected return, we would like to have historical data going a long way back.[7] In practice, we get around this problem by using the U.S. equity markets as a proxy for the world market portfolio. Due to the multinational nature of many U.S. companies and due to the enormous global diversity of asset holdings of U.S. companies, the U.S. equity market should be a fair proxy for the world asset market. So, we will take historical yearly returns of the U.S. equity markets and each year we will subtract off the 1-year return of a long-maturity Treasury bond (typically a 30-year bond) during that year. This produces a historical time series of $R_M - R_f$. (The R_M is proxied each year by the U.S. equity market return for that year, and R_f is proxied by the return produced the long Treasury bond during that year.) We can average this time series, which should produce a reasonable estimate of the going forward world market risk premium. This premium turns out to be approximately 6%. So now, we can calculate the risk premium for the stock of the food manufacturer.

$$R_A - R_f = 0.7 \times (6\%) = 4.2\%$$

The risk premium is 4.2%. If the current risk-free rate is 4.0% (this is the yield on a 30-year Treasury bond), we can calculate the expected return to an investor for holding the manufacturer's stock:

$$R_A - R_f = 4.2\%$$
$$R_A \quad = 4.2\% + R_f$$
$$= 4.2\% + 4.0\%$$
$$= 8.2\%$$

Thus, the expected return to an investor for holding this stock is 8.2%.

One might wonder why it is necessary to use the CAPM to calculate the expected return for an asset rather than simply averaging that asset's historical returns. The reason for this goes back to the discussion earlier about using historical returns to compute an expected market risk premium. Quite a lot of historical data is needed for the average to produce a good estimate (with low standard error) of the going forward expected return. However, the vast majority of assets such as publicly traded firms have not been in existence for a long time (or its returns have been available/observable for only a short period of time). For this reason, it is much more convenient to use historical data on the market (for which a long time series exists) and link the market to the asset for which we are interested in calculating an expected return. The critical information that allows this link is the β of the asset. Notice that the β only requires the calculation of second moments (correlation and volatilities); it does not require the calculation of an expected return (a first moment). A convenient statistical property about producing a good estimate (low standard error) for second moments is that its precision depends on the frequency of the historical data rather than the length of historical data (as first moments depend on). Therefore, as long as we use reasonably high frequency data (monthly or higher frequency) to calculate the β, we should be able to produce a good estimate for β. Thus, we have a way to produce good estimates for the market risk premium and the β of an asset with respect to the market. This is why we employ the CAPM to estimate expected returns for assets.

One might also wonder how to calculate a β for an asset. For many publicly traded securities such as equities, the β can be obtained from financial information services such as Bloomberg and Compustat. However, if it isn't available through such services, one can always calculate a β for an asset manually by running a regression of the asset's historical excess returns against the market's excess returns. The slope coefficient of such a regression is exactly the β that is needed in the CAPM.

5.6 The Cost of Capital for a Traded Asset

Now that we have discussed the CAPM, we are now ready to calculate the cost of capital, or discount rate, required in the present value equation, Equation 1. There are two situations to consider. First, we will consider the situation where we have an asset that is traded. If we consider the balance sheet representation for the asset, Figure 5.5, what this typically means is that the equity of the asset is traded.

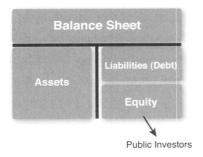

Figure 5.5 Balance sheet for an asset

When we implement the present value equation, we will match up the denominator to the numerator. What this means is that the cost of capital in the denominator will correspond to the riskiness of the cash flows in the numerator. We discuss this matching process and the details of implementing the present value equation in the next chapter. Therefore, in this section as well as the next one, we focus on calculating all three relevant costs of capital for a firm. These are the cost of equity capital (R_E), cost of debt capital (R_D) and the asset cost of capital (R_A). These are depicted in Figure 5.6.

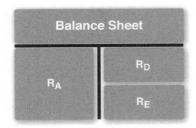

Figure 5.6 Costs of capital for the firm

We will go through the calculation of all three of these costs of capital via an example. Suppose that XYZ Corp. has a market value balance sheet as shown in Figure 5.7. The value of its equity is $500M. Its debt has a market value of $300M. Because the balance sheet must balance, debt plus equity must equal asset value. Therefore, its asset value is $800M.

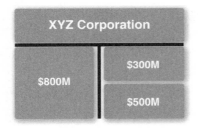

Figure 5.7 Balance sheet for XYZ Corp.

The cost of equity capital is fairly easy to calculate if XYZ is a market-traded firm. Essentially, we will calculate the cost of equity as we did in the previous section using the CAPM. Suppose that we find from financial information services or from our own regressions of XYZ's stock price data that XYZ's equity beta is 0.8. Then if the long bond yield is 4.0%, we have the following result for XYZ's cost of equity:

$$R_E = R_f + \beta_E (R_M - R_f)$$
$$= 4.0\% + 0.8(6\%)$$
$$= 8.8\%$$

We are assuming the same 6% world market risk premium, which we stipulated in the previous section. Therefore, the cost of equity is straightforward to calculate.

The cost of debt is a bit trickier. The first thing to realize is that for most firms, the market value of debt is difficult to obtain directly. This is because most firms either do not have publicly traded debt or have only a small fraction that is publicly traded. This is because most debt tends to be short/long-term bank debt and other forms of private debt. Therefore, the first question we are faced with is how to simply calculate the market value of debt for a firm. No matter what form of debt the firm has, this debt must be recorded on the firm's accounting balance sheet. Therefore, a commonly employed technique is to simply assume that the market value of debt is equal to the book value of debt recorded on the firm's accounting balance sheet. This is a reasonable assumption. When debt is issued, it is typically issued at par value—so that the value recorded on the accounting balance sheet is also the market value at the time of issuance. The question then is how big of a mistake might we make if we are looking at a firm's balance sheet, where all the debt on the books has been issued in the past. First, debt does not fluctuate in value as much as equities. This is because debt value is tied to interest rates, which are less volatile than equity prices. Second, interest rates tend to be mean-reverting, so that the market value of debt will probably fluctuate around par value. For these reasons, it can be argued that the error made by assuming that the market value of debt equals the book value of debt is not too bad. This is precisely how we arrived at the market value of debt for XYZ: $300M is the aggregate book value of this firm's debt, and we are assuming this to be its market value.

Knowing the market value of debt is the first step. We need to figure out the firm's cost of capital for this debt. Suppose that the firm's weighted average yield on this debt is Y_p. This yield is of course simply a *promised* yield (i.e., this is what the bond investor earns if the firm does not default). The cost of debt capital is the *expected* yield, which is what we need to calculate. The expected yield is a probability of default-weighted average of the promised yield and the yield a bond investor would get if the firm defaults:

$$Y_e = (1 - d)Y_p + dY_L \tag{11}$$

In this equation, Y_e is the expected yield, or cost of debt capital, which is what we are after. The letter d denotes the default probability of the firm, and Y_L denotes the yield, or loss rate, in case the firm defaults. Suppose that the weighted average yield of XYZ's debt is 5.5%. Suppose also that we know that XYZ's debt has an average debt rating of BBB+.[8] Then we can use information such as that given in Figures 5.8 and 5.9 to calculate the probability of default, d, and loss rate, Y_L. The information used to create these two figures is readily available from any of the major credit ratings agencies. From Figure 5.8, we can see that the average default rate for BBB-rated companies is 0.32% per year (1.6%/5 years). From Figure 5.9, if we assume that XYZ has mostly senior unsecured debt, the loss rate for XYZ's debt is $1 - 48\% = 52\%$. Therefore, we can now utilize Equation 11:

$$
\begin{aligned}
Y_e &= (1 - d)\, Y_p + dY_L \\
&= (1 - 0.32\%)\, 5.5\% + 0.32\%\, (-52\%) \\
&= 5.3\%
\end{aligned}
$$

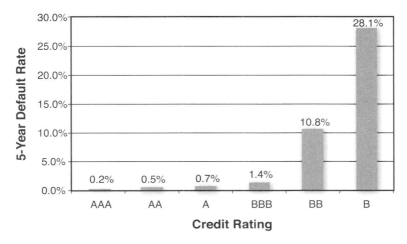

Figure 5.8 Default rates by credit rating

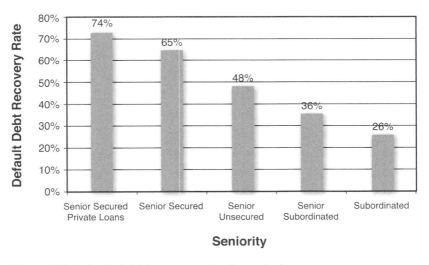

Figure 5.9 Defaulted debt recovery rates by seniority

Thus, the cost of debt capital, R_D, for XYZ is 5.3%. A "back of the envelope" technique that is sometimes employed to estimate the cost of debt capital is to simply assume that a firm's debt has a debt beta in the range of 0.1 to 0.5 and then to simply use the CAPM. The lower end of the beta range would be used for higher-quality (rated) firms, while the higher end of that range would be used for lower-quality firms. Let's try this with XYZ. Because XYZ is BBB+ rated (which is in the middle to upper-middle portion of the credit ratings range), suppose that we assume that XYZ's debt beta is roughly 0.2. We can now employ the CAPM:

$$R_D = R_f + \beta_D (R_M - R_f)$$
$$= 4.0\% + 0.2(6\%)$$
$$= 5.2\%$$

As you see, this quick-and-dirty approach produces a value that is close to the value we calculated through more precise means.

Now that we have calculated R_E and R_D, it is easy to calculate the asset cost of capital, R_A. Using Figure 5.6, and the fact that a balance sheet must balance, we have the following formula for the asset cost of capital for XYZ:

$$R_A = \frac{D}{D+E} R_D + \frac{E}{D+E} R_E \tag{12}$$

This equation states that the asset cost of capital is simply the weighted average of the cost of equity capital and the cost of debt capital. The weightings are simply the debt-to-total capital ratio and the equity-to-total capital ratio. The simple intuition of why this formula works derives from the balance sheet representation of a firm. This formula simply states that the asset cost of capital is the (market capitalization) weighted average of the debt cost of capital and the equity cost of capital.[9]

For XYZ, the market value of debt is $300M, and the market value of equity is $500M. Therefore, we can calculate its asset cost of capital:

$$R_A = \frac{D}{D+E} R_D + \frac{E}{D+E} R_E$$
$$= \frac{300}{300+500} 5.3\% + \frac{500}{300+500} 8.8\%$$
$$= 7.5\%$$

The asset cost of capital for XYZ is 7.5%. With this, we have calculated the costs of equity, debt, and asset capital for XYZ.

5.7 The Cost of Capital for a Nontraded Asset

We now take up the question of calculating the cost of equity capital, cost of debt capital, and asset cost of capital when the asset (specifically, its equity) is not traded (i.e., when it is a private asset). This is a typical situation. This not only applies to the valuation of private businesses but also the valuation of nearly any project. A project such as the introduction of a new product or a new marketing campaign is not traded. Therefore, the techniques discussed in the previous section become difficult to apply because we cannot measure the project's equity, debt, and asset values. Nevertheless, it is important to understand that the balance sheet depiction of Figure 5.5 still applies to the project; the difference is that we simply cannot observe the market values of the balance sheet components.

The standard approach to dealing with unobservable information in finance is to utilize traded comparables, whether those are comparable firms, comparable securities, or so on. We will utilize the same approach here. What we will do is find a comparable traded firm whose business (asset side of the balance sheet) is similar to the private asset that we are interested in calculating discount rates for.

We will continue the example from the previous section. Suppose that we are trying to calculate the costs of capital for ABC Corp. Unlike we did for XYZ Corp. discussed earlier, let's assume that ABC is nontraded. What this means is that we cannot observe its stock price movements through time. As a result, we cannot utilize the CAPM to determine a cost of equity capital as we did in the previous section. Instead, we will utilize the information that we have obtained from a comparable traded firm. We will assume that XYZ, the firm whose costs of capital we calculated above, is comparable to ABC. ABC's market value balance sheet is shown in Figure 5.10. ABC's equity has a market value of $1,200M, while its debt has a market value of $400M.[10] Its asset value is, therefore, $1,600M.[11]

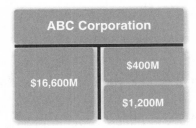

Figure 5.10 Balance sheet for ABC Co.

The key to determining ABC's costs of capital is XYZ. XYZ is a comparable firm. What this means is that the business that XYZ is in is similar to the business that ABC is in. In the language of finance, what this means is that the left-hand side of XYZ's balance sheet is similar to the left-hand side of ABC's balance sheet. Therefore, if the assets of the two balance sheets are similar, the riskiness of the assets in the two balance sheets must be similar as well. Finally, if the riskiness of the assets of ABC is similar to that of XYZ, the asset cost of capital for ABC should be the same as the asset cost of capital for XYZ. Thus, we've determined that the asset cost of capital for ABC must be 7.5%, the same as what we calculated above for XYZ.

We cannot use this same argument for determining the cost of equity and cost of debt for ABC because the riskiness of the right-hand sides of ABC's balance sheet and XYZ's balance sheet are very different. XYZ's debt ratio is 38%, while ABC's debt ratio is 25%. The lower debt ratio for ABC means that it has a lower probability of defaulting. The lower probability of default implies that both the cost of debt and the cost of equity for ABC must be lower, reflecting the lower level of risk.

We can go through either of the approaches previously described to determine the cost of debt for ABC. To keep things simple, we will assume that the lower riskiness means that the debt beta for ABC is slightly lower than average, at around 0.15. This translates into a cost of debt of

$$
\begin{aligned}
R_D &= R_f + \beta_D\,(R_M - R_f) \\
&= 4.0\% + 0.15(6\%) \\
&= 4.9\%
\end{aligned}
$$

We can now figure out the cost of equity by applying Equation 12 again. The difference now is that rather than calculating the cost of assets, the unknown variable is the cost of equity. So, we will solve for that instead:

$$
R_A = \frac{D}{D+E} R_D + \frac{E}{D+E} R_E
$$

$$
7.5\% = \frac{400}{400+1200} 4.9\% + \frac{1000}{400+1200} R_E
$$

We can now solve this for the R_E, the cost of equity for XYZ:

$$
\begin{aligned}
R_E &= \frac{D+E}{E} R_A - \frac{D}{E} R_D \\
&= \frac{400+1200}{1200} 7.5\% - \frac{400}{1200} 4.9\% \\
&= 8.4\%
\end{aligned}
$$

Thus, ABC's cost of equity is 8.4%, which is less than XYZ's cost of equity calculated earlier of 8.8%. Because ABC has less leverage than XYZ, its equity is less risky, and therefore the cost of its equity is lower. The key step in calculating ABC's cost of equity was inverting the asset cost of capital formula, Equation 12, and solving for the cost of equity rather than the cost of assets.

To summarize, by using a comparable traded firm, we can calculate the costs of capital for a nontraded firm. The cost of assets for the nontraded firm will be the same as that of the traded firm because they are in similar businesses. Because we can safely assume that the book value of debt and market value of debt are fairly close, the cost of debt can be obtained through the same methodologies described in the previous section. Finally, the cost of equity can be obtained by inverting the asset cost of capital formula, Equation 12, and solving for the cost of equity of the nontraded firm.

5.8 The Asset Cost of Capital Formula

We mentioned when we first stated the formula for the asset cost of capital, Equation 12, that the derivation of this formula is not as simple as one might think. This section shows the details of the derivation of this formula. This will also give us an opportunity to introduce the notion of an interest tax shield and how this fits into the balance sheet representation of a firm.

If we consider the balance sheet representations of the firm and the costs of capital for a firm, Figures 5.5 and 5.6, there is an important element that is not explicitly stated in these figures. Specifically, it is the fact that the presence of debt on a balance sheet introduces a tax shield into the balance sheet. This is because the interest expense on debt is tax deductible. The tax deduction results in an increase in cash flows for the firm by reducing the firm's tax expense. Because this is a perpetual increase in cash flow, the value of this tax shield is worth much more than the increase in cash flow in any given year.

Figure 5.11 shows how the balance sheet view of a firm looks with this tax shield value included. The value of the tax shield, TS, shows up on the left-hand side of the balance sheet. Therefore, the assets are now split into two components. The first is the operating assets, OA, of the firm, which are used to derive the revenues for the business. The second is the tax shield.[12] The two together sum to form the total assets, A, of the firm.

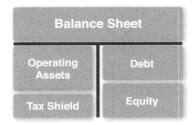

Figure 5.11 Balance sheet with tax shield

Based on Figure 5.11, we can now write a relationship between the costs of capital for a firm:

$$\frac{OA}{OA+TS}R_{OA} + \frac{TS}{OA+TS}R_{TS} = \frac{D}{D+E}R_{D} + \frac{E}{D+E}R_{E}$$

(13)

The discount rate of the tax shield is a function of the debt policy followed by the firm. At this point, we will discuss two types of debt policy: a fixed debt *level* policy and a fixed debt *ratio* policy. A fixed debt level indicates that regardless of what happens to the size of the firm's assets and equity the firm intends to keep the same dollar amount of debt on the balance sheet going into the future. A fixed debt ratio policy indicates that the firm will maintain the same proportion of debt to assets on the balance sheet. Thus, with a fixed debt ratio as the level of assets increases or decreases, the debt level will increase or decrease, respectively, in such a way that the ratio of debt to assets remains the same into the future. Notice that a fixed debt ratio policy also implies that the ratio of debt to equity on the balance will also necessarily remain the same into the future.

We first take up the case of a fixed debt ratio. In this case, the amount of the tax shield is directly related to the level of debt on the balance sheet. The more debt there is on the balance sheet, the greater the tax shield. The less debt there is, the lower the tax shield. Therefore, the variability of the tax shield is directly proportional to the variability of the debt level. This in turn means that the riskiness of the tax shield, and therefore its discount rate, is directly proportional to the variability of the debt level. However, the debt level is tied to the asset level, and therefore the variability of the debt level is equal to the variability of the asset level. We can now tie these two pieces together. The variability (risk) of the tax shield must be equal to the variability (risk) of the asset level because the debt level is proportional to the asset level. Thus, the discount rate of the tax shield is equal to the discount rate of the assets: $R_{TS} = R_A$.

If the amount of the tax shield is small relative to the amount of operating assets in the firm, then the operating asset value is approximately equal to the asset value, $OA = A$. As a result, we can simply denote OA as A. Therefore, we can rewrite Equation 13 as

$$\frac{OA}{OA+TS}R_A + \frac{TS}{OA+TS}R_A = \frac{D}{D+E}R_D + \frac{E}{D+E}R_E \tag{14}$$

We can now combine the two fractions on the left-hand side of this equation:

$$\frac{OA+TS}{OA+TS}R_A = \frac{D}{D+E}R_D + \frac{E}{D+E}R_E \tag{15}$$

Of course, $\dfrac{OA+TS}{OA+TS}=1$, and therefore we have

$$R_A = \frac{D}{D+E}R_D + \frac{E}{D+E}R_E \tag{16}$$

This is precisely the same formula as stated earlier in Equation 12. However, we see from the careful derivation of this equation that it only applies when the firm is following a policy of maintaining a constant debt ratio.

Now let's consider the other debt policy: Suppose that the firm decides to maintain a fixed debt level rather than a fixed debt ratio. We start with Equation 13 again. However, with a fixed debt level, we can figure out the value of the tax shield precisely by utilizing Equation 1 to determine its present value. If we assume that the firm faces a tax rate of τ on its profits, then each year $1 of interest increases the after-tax cash flow by $1 \times \tau$. This is because $1 of interest reduces earnings before taxes (EBT) by $1 and thereby shields $1 of EBT from taxation. If the tax rate is, for example, 35%, that $1 reduction of net income produces an extra $0.35 of earnings after taxes, or net income. So, each dollar of interest expense increases after-tax cash flow by τ dollars each year. We can use this information to calculate the total present value of the tax shield.

If the debt is at par value, the interest rate on the debt is equal to its market yield; therefore, the interest rate on the debt is R_D. For simplicity, we will assume that interest is paid annually. The total annual interest payment that the firm makes on its debt is $R_D D$, the interest rate times the principal amount of the debt. Because the debt level is fixed, this is the annual payment the firm makes on its debt into perpetuity. From above, we know that for every $1 of interest paid, the firm gets a tax shield of τ. Therefore, the annual tax shield into perpetuity is equal to $R_D D \tau$.

We can now use the present value formula, Equation 1, to calculate the present value of these annual tax shield benefits. The annual tax shield cash flow is given by $R_D D \tau$. The riskiness of this tax shield is equal to the riskiness of the debt because the debt level is fixed (unlike with a fixed debt ratio where the debt level varies with the asset level). Therefore, the discount rate on the annual tax shield is simply the discount rate on the debt, R_D. The total tax shield value is then given by

$$TS = \frac{R_D D_\tau}{1+R_D} + \frac{R_D D_\tau}{(1+R_D)^2} + \frac{R_D D_\tau}{(1+R_D)^3} + \cdots \tag{17}$$

It is easy to simplify the right-hand side of this equation:[13]

$$TS = D\tau \tag{18}$$

We have therefore calculated the value of the tax shield. We can now go to Equation 13 and make two substitutions into this equation. First, we can replace TS with $D\tau$ in the numerator of the second term. Second, we can replace R_{TS} with R_D because we know that the discount rate of the tax shield is simply the cost of debt (due to the fixed debt level policy). Third, we know that a balance sheet must balance, so we know that OA + TS = D + E. Therefore, we can replace OA + TS with D + E. These substitutions leave us with the following equation:

$$\frac{OA}{D+E}R_{OA} + \frac{D\tau}{D+E}R_D = \frac{D}{D+E}R_D + \frac{E}{D+E}R_E \qquad (19)$$

We can move $\dfrac{D_\tau}{D+E}R_D$ to the right-hand side and consolidate terms.

$$\frac{OA}{D+E}R_{OA} = \frac{D-D_\tau}{D+E}R_D + \frac{E}{D+E}R_E \qquad (20)$$

$$= \frac{D}{D+E}R_D(1-\tau) + \frac{E}{D+E}R_E \qquad (21)$$

As we did earlier with a fixed debt ratio policy, if we again assume that the tax shield value is small compared to the value of operating assets, then the operating asset value is approximately equal to the asset value, $OA \approx A$. We can replace OA on the left-hand side with A:

$$\frac{A}{D+E}R_A = \frac{D-D_\tau}{D+E}R_D + \frac{E}{D+E}R_E \qquad (22)$$

$$R_A = \frac{D}{D+E}R_D(1-\tau) + \frac{E}{D+E}R_E \qquad (23)$$

The second line follows because $\dfrac{A}{D+E}=1$. Thus, we have derived the asset cost of capital formula, Equation 23 in the case where the firm is following a fixed debt level policy. In this case, we use the after-tax cost of debt on the right-hand side of the formula. Notice that although it is very close to the asset cost of capital formula in the case of fixed debt ratio, Equation 16, it is nevertheless not the same. In Equation 16, we use the pretax cost of debt.

In conclusion, we have to know which situation we are in before applying an asset cost of capital formula to a firm. If a firm is following a fixed debt *ratio* policy, we use the pretax cost of debt in the asset cost of capital formula. If a firm is following a fixed debt *level* policy, we use the after-tax cost of debt in this formula. In most cases, firms follow a policy of maintaining a fixed debt ratio, and therefore one would typically use Equation 16 for determining the asset cost of capital.[14] This is precisely what we did in the examples in this chapter where we calculated firms' costs of capital.

Endnotes

1 By *risk free*, we mean that in the case of this security, if you pay $95 and purchase this T-bill, you will receive the principal of $100 for sure in one year. Therefore, there is no possibility of default. Our working assumption throughout this book is that U.S. government-backed securities are the safest ones available in the entire investment universe. Therefore, we will treat all such securities as being free of risk over the life of those securities.

2 Note that this is not the same thing as a credit spread. The credit spread is the difference in promised returns rather than expected returns between the corporate bond and Treasury bill. The credit spread in this example would be

$$(\frac{\$100}{\$93} - 1) - (\frac{\$100}{\$95} - 1) = 2.26\%$$

The credit spread does not factor in the possibility of default in the calculation of future payoffs. (Both payoffs in the earlier calculation assume $100 received at maturity.) Therefore, the credit spread is always higher than the expected return for bonds.

3 We hope this is fairly intuitive to the reader, as well. This principle is rooted in the microeconomics concept of concave investor preferences, which we do not delve into in this book.

4 We can always make qualitative statements such as "the company is unlikely to default," but attaching a specific number to the probability of default is impossible.

5 Note that we are not taking into effect compounding here. The 24% is simply a quoting mechanism and not an expected return. The expected return is 2% per month, and 24% per annum is simply a way to quote the 2% per month.

6 Note that $w_A + w_B = 1$. So, we could also have stated the two weights as w_A and $1 - w_A$.

7 This is due to a statistical characteristic of the first moments of any random variable, which is how we are modeling asset prices. To generate a reasonably accurate estimate (i.e., one with a low standard error) of the first moment of a random variable, a very long time series is needed.

8 We are using S&P credit ratings here. A rough equivalent in terms of Moody's ratings would be Baa1.

9 Although this looks like it derives easily from the balance sheet representation of a firm, it is actually a bit tricky. This is due to the fact that debt on the right-hand side of the balance sheet introduces a tax shield into the balance sheet. We derive this formula more rigorously in the last section, Section 5.8, "The Asset Cost of Capital Formula."

10 One can assume that this market value was calculated as it was done for XYZ previously; i.e., this is the book value of its aggregate long-term debt

11 Note that while we are assuming that we can determine the market value of equity today (we discuss in the next chapter how to do this), we do not know the historical movement of this equity price. It is because of this lack of time series information

that we cannot calculate its equity beta and, therefore, its equity cost of capital directly.

12 Because the tax shield does not directly contribute to business revenue, we do not consider this asset as part of the operating assets.

13 We use the following general formula for the summation of an infinite series:

$$V = a + a(1+r) + a(1+r)^2 + a(1+r)^3 + \dots$$

$$\frac{a}{1-r}$$

14 Notable exceptions include cases such as leveraged buyouts where a firm is following a policy of reducing debt according to a specific debt repayment schedule.

6

Putting It All Together: Valuation Frameworks

6.1 Introduction

We are now at the final stage where we can put all of the pieces in the previous chapters together to do a valuation of any asset, whether that asset is a firm or a project, or whether that asset is public or private. The main tool for doing this valuation is the present value relation:

$$Value_0 = \frac{E(CF_1)}{1+r} + \frac{E(CF_2)}{(1+r)^2} + \frac{E(CF_3)}{(1+r)^3} + \dots \quad (1)$$

where $E(CF_1)$, $E(CF_2)$, and so on are expected future cash flows, r denotes a discount rate, and $Value_0$ is the value of the project that we are trying to measure. In the previous chapters, we discussed how to calculate the cash flows and the discount rates. Each year we construct projected financial statements for the project or firm that we are interested in valuing. From these financial projections we then calculate free cash flows:

$$FCF = EBIAT - \Delta NWC - \text{CapEx} + \text{Depr} \quad (2)$$

The free cash flows from this equation are used as the expected future cash flows in Equation 1.

The discount rate is calculated by determining the riskiness of the free cash flows. The discount rate under each cash flow compensates for the riskiness of that cash flow. Because free cash flows are coming from the left side of the balance sheet of the asset we are trying to value, the discount rate is simply the asset cost of capital. To determine the asset cost of capital, we need to use a combination of comparable assets, the CAPM

$$R_A - R_f = \beta A (R_M - R_f) \tag{3}$$

and the asset cost of capital formula:

$$R_A = \frac{D}{D+E} R_D + \frac{E}{D+E} R_E \tag{4}$$

We have two final concepts to discuss to have a fully developed valuation methodology. The first is how to deal with the effects of debt financing, specifically the tax shield. The second is how to compute the sum of an infinite number of cash flows as we apply Equation 1.

Figure 6.1 depicts the balance sheet view of the asset we are trying to value. The presence of debt on the right side of the balance sheet and the fact that the interest on debt is tax deductible imply that a tax shield is created on the left side of the balance sheet. From Equation 2, the free cash flows that we calculate for the asset are independent of the capital structure and therefore do not capture the value of this tax shield. So, we must incorporate the value of the tax shield in another way. In this section, we present three valuation approaches for executing Equation 1. The valuation approaches differ primarily in how this tax shield is incorporated. The adjusted present value (APV) approach treats this tax shield as a separate asset and calculates its value by applying Equation 1 a second time—this time to value the tax shield. The weighted average cost of capital (WACC) approach incorporates the tax shield benefit into the discount rate. The flow to equity (FTE) approach utilizes cash flows to equity rather than free cash flows. Therefore, it deducts the interest payment in the process of calculating cash flows, thus incorporating the tax shield value in the cash flows.

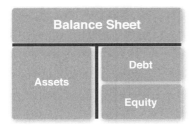

Figure 6.1 Balance sheet

The second issue that we have is how to deal with potentially an infinite number of terms in Equation 1. For some assets, the cash flows will be expected to cease after a finite number of years. In these cases, we would simply apply Equation 1 out to the number of years until the cash flows end. However, many assets, such as a firm, will have expected cash flows out to perpetuity. In these cases, we have an infinite number of cash flows and, therefore, an infinite number of terms in computing Equation 1. The general approach for dealing with this situation is to truncate Equation 1 at some point and have a final term, a *terminal value*, that captures the remaining infinite number of cash flow terms. This section introduces several techniques to calculate this terminal value.

6.2 APV

Figure 6.1 shows that a valuation of the balance sheet must somehow incorporate the tax shield that arises from having debt on the right side of the balance sheet. The APV methodology proposes to do this in two steps. First, we value the operating assets using the free cash flows that they generate and calculating the present value of these free cash flows. Then, the tax shield is valued separately by calculating the present value of the interest tax shield that arises each year due to the tax deductibility of interest payments. Therefore, the APV approach can be stated as

$$APV = PV \text{ of Operating Assets} + PV \text{ of Tax Shield} \qquad (5)$$

The present value of operating assets is calculated by discounting the free cash flows that these assets generate. Because it is the assets that generate these free cash flows, the discount rate that appropriately compensates for the riskiness of the free cash flows is the cost of assets, R_A.[1]

$$APV_0 = \frac{FCF_1}{1+R_A} + \frac{FCF_2}{(1+R_A)^2} + \frac{FCF_3}{(1+R_A)^3} + \ldots + PV \text{ of Tax Shield}$$
$$(6)$$

In the numerators, we have dropped the expectation term, but it should be understood that all of the free cash flows occur in the future, and therefore, FCF_1, FCF_2, ... are all expected free cash flows.

We can similarly restate the calculation of the tax shield present value. Suppose that the amount of debt on the balance sheet in future periods is denoted as D1, D2, ... The interest rate on this debt is given by R_D. Therefore, in year n, there is an expected interest payment of $D_n \times R_D$. Because this interest payment is tax deductible, the tax authorities effectively subsidize this payment by an amount equal to the tax rate, τ, multiplied by the interest payment. Therefore, the tax shield generated in year n would be $\tau D_n R_D$. With this result, we can now state the general formula for the APV of an asset:

$$APV_0 = \left. \frac{FCF_1}{1+R_A} + \frac{FCF_2}{(1+R_A)^2} + \frac{FCF_3}{(1+R_A)^3} + \ldots \right\} PV \text{ of Operating Assets}$$
$$(7)$$

$$\left. + \frac{\tau D_1 R_D}{1+R_D} + \frac{\tau D_2 R_D}{(1+R_D)^2} + \frac{\tau D_3 R_D}{(1+R_D)^3} + \ldots \right\} PV \text{ of Tax Shield} \qquad (8)$$

As an example of the tax shield calculation, suppose that we have a project that we are trying to value with a fixed level of debt, D. Therefore, the level of debt is expected to remain at the level D forever. We will calculate the present value of the tax shield in this case:

$$\text{PV of Tax Shield} = \frac{\tau D_1 R_D}{1 + R_D} + \frac{\tau D_2 R_D}{(1 + R_D)^2} + \frac{\tau D_3 R_D}{(1 + R_D)^3} + \ldots$$

$$= \frac{\tau D R_D}{1 + R_D} + \frac{\tau D R_D}{(1 + R_D)^2} + \frac{\tau D R_D}{(1 + R_D)^3} + \ldots$$

$$= \tau D R_D \left[\frac{1}{1 + R_D} + \frac{1}{(1 + R_D)^2} + \frac{1}{(1 + R_D)^3} + \ldots \right]$$

It is easy to show mathematically that

$$\left[\frac{1}{1 + R_D} + \frac{1}{(1 + R_D)^2} + \frac{1}{(1 + R_D)^3} + \ldots \right] = \frac{1}{R_D}$$

Therefore, we have the result that in the case of a fixed level of debt D into perpetuity with a tax rate of τ

$$\text{PV of Tax Shield} = \tau D R_D \frac{1}{R_D}$$

$$= \tau D$$

We show examples of how to utilize the APV approach shortly.

6.3 Terminal Value

We have one final issue to deal with before we can utilize the APV approach. Equation 7 is an infinite sum. While some assets have finite lives, many assets go on into perpetuity, such as a business or real estate. Therefore, to value such perpetual assets, one would have to present value an infinite number of free cash flows to evaluate Equation 7. In most cases, it will not be feasible to find an exact solution to this infinite sum as we did in the previous section in the case of valuing a tax shield with a fixed level of debt. The standard way of dealing with this issue is to truncate the infinite sum at some point[2] and add one additional term, called a *terminal value,* to capture the remaining summation terms:

$$APV = \frac{FCF_1}{1+R_A} + \frac{FCF_2}{(1+R_A)^2} + \frac{FCF_3}{(1+R_A)^3} + \ldots \frac{FCF_n}{(1+R_A)^n} + \frac{TV}{(1+R_A)^n}$$

+PV of Tax Shield (9)

The term *TV* in the numerator of the last free cash flow term denotes the terminal value of the asset at the end of n years. In this section, we present three alternative methods for computing this terminal value: the liquidation value, the growing perpetuity value, and the multiples value.

6.3.1 Liquidation Value

To use liquidation value as the terminal value, one assumes that the asset being valued is liquidated at the end of the nth year in Equation 9. In this case, one can separate the assets being liquidated into net working capital and PP&E. Net working capital can typically be liquidated at full book value, whereas PP&E is usually liquidated at a gain or loss relative to book value. If there is a gain/loss on the liquidation of net working capital or PP&E, this gain/loss is taxable. (In the case of a loss, the loss generates a tax credit.) It is important to net out any tax effects from the liquidation value. Thus, the terminal value utilizing the liquidation value approach is simply the value recovered from liquidating the net working capital plus the value recovered from liquidating PP&E plus any tax effects from any gains/losses (relative to book value) from liquidating this net working capital and PP&E.

We will now demonstrate how to use the APV approach with the terminal value calculated by using the liquidation value approach.

Consider the project in which ABC Co. was thinking about investing, described at the end of Chapter 4, "Free Cash Flows." The free cash flows for this project were calculated at the end of Chapter 4 in Figure 4.6. We will value this project, a new product introduction, to determine whether ABC Co. should undertake this project.

Figure 6.2 shows the results of applying the APV approach to this project. The current time is at the end of 2013. We assume that we have checked comparables and gone through the cost of capital calculation process described in the previous chapter to arrive at an asset cost of capital for the project of 11%.[3] After determining free cash flows (FCF), a terminal value (TV) is calculated in 2020. It is assumed that the manufacturing plant that was built for the project in 2014 and 2015 can be sold at the end of 2020 for $5M. However, because the plant has been depreciated down to zero book value, this sale represents a gain and ABC Co. would have to pay tax at ABC's marginal corporate tax rate (25%) on this gain. Therefore, the liquidation value is $5M × (1 − 25%) = $3.75M. The free cash flows and terminal value are added together and discounted at the 11% asset cost of capital rate to produce a present value ($PV[FCF + TV]$) for each year.

Figure 6.2 APV of Project by ABC Co. Using Liquidation Value

Financial Projections ($000s)

	2013	2014	2015	2016	2017	2018	2019	2020
Sales				71,400	82,800	82,800	43,400	21,600
COGS				50,694	58,788	58,788	30,814	15,336
SG&A				7,140	8,280	8,280	4,340	2,160
EBIT				13,566	15,732	15,732	8,246	4,104
EBIAT				10,175	11,799	11,799	6,185	3,078
NWC			17,850	20,700	20,700	10,850	5,400	0
Change in NWC			17,850	2,850	0		–5,450	–5,400
CapEx		20,000	20,000					
Depr				8,000	8,000	8,000	8,000	8,000
FCF		–20,000	–37,850	15,325	19,799	19,799	19,635	16,478
TV								3,750

Financial Projections ($000s)

	2013	2014	2015	2016	2017	2018	2019	2020
R(A) = 11%								
PV(FCF + TV)		−18,018	−30,720	11,205	13,042	11,750	10,497	9,743
Debt Level		20,000	40,000	40,000	40,000	40,000	40,000	40,000
R(D) = 6%								
Interest Payment		1,200	2,400	2,400	2,400	2,400	2,400	2,400
Tax Shield CF		300	600	600	600	600	600	600
PV(Tax Shield CFs)		283	534	504	475	448	423	399
APV	10,566							

In the APV approach, the tax shield value of the project must now be calculated. We assume that the $20M investments in 2014 and 2015 to build the manufacturing facility are financed by debt. Therefore, the debt level for the project is at $20M at the end of 2014, and $40M at the end of 2015 and onward. We assume a cost of debt ($R[D]$) of 6%. This leads to interest payments of $1.2M in 2014 and $2.4M in 2015 and beyond. These interest payments produce a yearly tax shield of the interest payment times the tax rate (25%). The present value of each of these tax shields is computed by discounting at the cost of debt of 6%.

The sum of the present values of the free cash flows, terminal value, and the tax shield cash flows produces an APV of $16.4M. Therefore, by investing in this project, ABC Co. would derive $16.4M of net positive value (which would accrue to its equity holders).

6.3.2 Growing Perpetuity Value

Instead of the liquidation value approach, we can arrive at the terminal value by determining the growing perpetuity value of the infinite sum of discounted free cash flows. This approach works well in the situation where the variability of the free cash flows decreases and the free cash flows settle into a smooth growing pattern. In this case, the terminal value is defined by the following equation:

$$TV = \frac{FCF_n(1+g)}{1+R_A} + \frac{FCF_n(1+g)^2}{(1+R_A)^2} + \frac{FCF_n(1+g)^3}{(1+R_A)^3} + \ldots \tag{10}$$

In this equation, the free cash flows have settled down to a smooth growth rate of g. Because the free cash flows are growing at a constant rate g, we can solve for the terminal value in closed form. We first multiply both sides of this equation by $(1 + g) / (1 + R_A)$:

$$TV\frac{1+g}{1+R_A} = \frac{FCF_n(1+g)^2}{(1+R_A)^2} + \frac{FCF_n(1+g)^3}{(1+R_A)^3} + \frac{FCF_n(1+g)^4}{(1+R_A)^4} + \dots$$

(11)

We then subtract this equation from the first one. Because all of the terms on the right side of Equation 11 are present on the right side of Equation 10, this subtraction leaves us with a much simpler equation:

$$TV - TV\frac{1+g}{1+R_A} = \frac{FCF_n(1+g)}{1+R_A}$$

(12)

We can now solve this equation for TV on the left side:

$$TV = \frac{\dfrac{FCF_n(1+g)}{1+R_A}}{1 - \dfrac{1+g}{1+R_A}}$$

(13)

This expression can be simplified to

$$TV = \frac{FCF_n(1+g)}{R_A - g}$$

(14)

Equation 14 provides a simple formula for calculating a terminal value once the cash flows have settled to a growing perpetuity. As a result, this formula is known as the growing perpetuity formula, and the terminal value is known as the growing perpetuity value.

A special case of this formula is the situation when the free cash flows are not growing, so that the free cash flows go on forever at a fixed level (i.e., a perpetuity). In this case, $g = 0$, so that the formula simply becomes the following perpetuity formula for terminal value:

$$TV = \frac{FCF_n}{R_A}$$

(15)

It is important to note here that for the growing perpetuity formula to work, the growth rate of the free cash flows, g, must be less than the asset cost of capital, R_A.[4] We demonstrate how to implement APV with the growing perpetuity approach for calculating a terminal value by valuing ABC Co. today (end of 2013). The free cash flows for ABC were calculated at the end of Chapter 4 in Figure 4.5. In Figure 6.3, we calculate the enterprise value[5] and equity value of ABC utilizing APV. We first make one small change to the cash flows from Figure 4.5. In Figure 4.5 we determined ABC Co.'s free cash flows to be negative every year. This is primarily because of ABC's large amount of capital expenditures; they are currently investing heavily in their businesses to grow them. Of course, to survive, ABC has to produce positive free cash flows in the long run. We accelerate this process and assume that in Figure 6.3 the heavy capital expenditures are finished and that the only ongoing capital expenditures are simply to maintain the business at a normal growth rate. Thus, capital expenditures are reduced, and the resulting free cash flows (FCF) in 2015 and beyond are now positive.

Figure 6.3 APV of ABC Co. Using Growing Perpetuity

Financial Projections ($MM)

	2013	2014	2015	2016	2017	2018
Net Revenue		11,664	12,831	14,114	15,525	17,077
COGS		8,940	9,834	10,818	11,899	13,089
R&D		298	328	361	397	437
SG&A		1,234	1,358	1,494	1,643	1,807
Other Expenses		304	335	368	405	445
EBIT		887	976	1,073	1,181	1,299
Taxes		188	207	228	251	276
EBIAT		699	768	845	930	
NWC		53	58	64	71	78
Change in NWC		5	5	6	6	7
PP&E (BoY)		8,895	9,785	10,274	10,788	11,327

Financial Projections ($MM)

	2013	2014	2015	2016	2017	2018
Capital Expenditures		1,383	1,032	1,084	1,138	1,195
Depreciation		494	543	570	599	629
PP&E (EoY)		9,785	10,274	10,788	11,327	11,893
FCF		−196	274	326	384	−573
TV (g = 4%)						−11,927
R(A) = 9%						
PV(FCF + TV)		−180	231	252	272	−8,124
Debt Level		3,584	3,851	4,143	4,463	4,812
R(D) = 6%						
Interest Payment		215	231	249	268	289
Tax Shield CF		46	49	53	57	61
TV of Tax Shield						1,022
PV(Tax Shield CFs + TV)		43	44	44	45	810
Enterprise Value	**−6,564**					
Debt Value	**3,339**					
Equity Value	**−9,903**					

Once the free cash flows have been calculated, a terminal value needs to be determined. We calculate a terminal value (TV) at the end of 2018 using the growing perpetuity formula, Equation 14. We assume an asset cost of capital of 9% has been derived[6] and that a perpetual growth rate of 4% has been determined. The growth rate assumption is an important one. Because this growth is expected to occur forever, we must be careful not to use too high of a growth rate; otherwise, our calculations would be assuming that ABC would grow faster than the world economy forever (which would implicitly assume that ABC would eventually become the world economy). Historically, the world economy has had a *real* growth rate of about 1.5%.

Long-run inflation for the world historically has been about 2.5%. Therefore, the historical long-run nominal growth rate of the world economy has been about 4%, which is the number we use for the growth rate in Equation 14. The terminal value is therefore

$$TV = \frac{FCF_n(1+g)}{R_A - g}$$
$$= \frac{\$449M\,(1+4\%)}{9\% - 4\%}$$
$$= \$9,348M$$

We can now calculate the present value each year for the sum of the cash flow and terminal value each year.

To finish the APV calculation, we now need to calculate the present value of the tax shields. The debt levels (Debt Level) are calculated from Figure 3.1.1 (which contains the pro forma financials for ABC) as the sum of long-term debt and long-term liabilities. The cost of debt is assumed to be 6%. The product of the debt level each year and the interest rate produces the interest payment for each year. The tax shield for each year (Tax Shield CF) is simply the product of the interest payment and the corporate tax rate (21.24% from Figure 3.1.1). Because the tax shield cash flows go on forever, we need to calculate a terminal value in 2018 for the tax shields as well. We do this by assuming that the debt level stays fixed at the 2018 level forever; therefore, we can use the perpetuity formula with no growth, Equation 15. This produces a terminal value of $61M / 6% = $1,022M. We can now calculate the present value each year for the sum of the tax shield cash flow and terminal value each year.

The APV (Enterprise Value) is simply the sum of the present values of the free cash flows and terminal value and the present values of the tax shields and tax shield terminal value. This is equal to $7,928M for ABC. To calculate the equity value, we just need to subtract the current debt value from the enterprise value. The current debt value (end of 2013) from Figure 3.1.1 is the sum of the long-term debt and other long-term liabilities, which equals $3,339M. Therefore, the equity value for ABC is $7,928M – $3,339M = $4,589M.

6.3.3 *Multiples Value*

Finally, instead of the liquidation value approach or using a growing perpetuity value approach, we can calculate the terminal value by determining the market value of the asset at the point of terminal value calculation. We would use the method of multiples value to determine this market value.

The multiples approach is a common way to calculate a terminal value. The concept behind this approach is to calculate a terminal value by simply computing a market value for the asset side of the balance sheet at the terminal value point. This market value is determined by looking at the market values of comparable assets today and proportionately impute a similar valuation for the terminal value of the asset we are trying to value. We do this by assuming that the asset we are valuing will have a terminal value multiple that is equal to that of the multiples of the comparables.

It is easiest to understand this approach through an example. Figure 6.4 contains the valuation of ABC that we did previously in Figure 6.3. The APV process and the numbers are the same. In Figure 6.4, however, we assume that the terminal value of free cash flows (TV) is calculated as a multiple rather than as a growing perpetuity. To calculate this terminal value, therefore, we need to determine what the appropriate multiple should be. Figure 6.5 contains a table of comparable firms and their enterprise value multiples based on current (2013) market values. For example, the EBIT multiple of 6.4 for DEF Corp. indicates that DEF's current enterprise value is 6.4 times the EBIT it produced for the previous year. Similarly, the EBITDA multiple indicates the ratio of enterprise value to EBITDA.[7] The B/M multiple is referred to as a *book-to-market* multiple, and it denotes the ratio of the book value of assets to the market value of assets (enterprise value). We will use an EBIT multiple to calculate the terminal value for ABC in Figure 6.4. Because all the firms listed in Figure 6.5 are comparables to ABC, we will simply use their average EBIT multiple, 7.8, and assume that it applies to ABC in 2018. So, we can now calculate the terminal value for ABC in 2018 as 7.8 times ABC's 2018 EBIT, which is calculated earlier in Figure 6.4 as \$1,299M. Therefore, the terminal value is 7.8 × \$1, 299M = \$10,130M.

Figure 6.4 APV of ABC Co. Using EBIT Multiple

Financial Projections (\$MM)

	2013	2014	2015	2016	2017	2018
Net Revenue		11,664	12,831	14,114	15,525	17,077
COGS		8,940	9,834	10,818	11,899	13,089
R&D		298	328	361	397	437
SG&A		1,234	1,358	1,494	1,643	1,807
Other Expenses		304	335	368	405	445
EBIT		887	976	1,073	1,181	1,299
Taxes		188	207	228	251	276
EBIAT		699	768	845	930	
NWC		53	58	64	71	78
Change in NWC		5	5	6	6	7
PP&E (BoY)		8,895	9,785	10,274	10,788	11,327
Capital Expenditures		1,383	1,032	1,084	1,138	1,195
Depreciation		494	543	570	599	629
PP&E (EoY)		9,785	10,274	10,788	11,327	11,893
FCF		−196	274	326	384	−573
TV						10,130
R(A) = 9%						
PV(FCF + TV)		−180	231	252	272	6,211
Debt Level		3,584	3,851	4,143	4,463	4,812
R(D) = 6%						

Financial Projections ($MM)

	2013	2014	2015	2016	2017	2018
Interest Payment		215	231	249	268	289
Tax Shield CF		46	49	53	57	61
TV of Tax Shield						0
PV(Tax Shield CFs + TV)		43	44	44	45	46

Enterprise Value	7,008
Debt Value	3,339
Equity Value	3,669

Figure 6.5 Enterprise Value Multiples

	EBIT	EBITDA	B/M
Company	**Multiple**	**Multiple**	**Multiple**
DEF Corp.	6.4	4.7	1.1
GHI Corp.	7.3	5.2	0.9
JKL Corp.	10.7	8.7	2.3
MNO Corp.	6.5	4.8	1.3
PQR Corp.	8.2	7.4	1.9
Average	**7.8**	**6.2**	**1.5**

To finish the APV calculation, we need to determine the tax shield value. This is done in exactly the same way and using the same numbers as in Figure 6.3. The only difference is that a terminal value of tax shield cash flows does not need to be included. This is because we have already captured this in the terminal value of free cash flows. The multiples of comparable firms in Figure 6.5 use market values, which naturally include all tax shields. So, for example, DEF's EBIT multiple is the ratio of DEF's enterprise value to EBIT where the enterprise value is the total asset value of DEF including the tax shield value. Therefore, when we applied an EBIT multiple to calculate ABC's free cash flow terminal value, we also captured the tax shield terminal value. So, we do not need to do a separate tax shield terminal value.

The resulting enterprise value for ABC using the multiples approach is $7,673M and ABC's equity value is $4,334M.

The obvious drawback with the multiples approach is that it assumes that the multiples that are present in the marketplace today will apply in the future at the point in time we truncate the free cash flow calculation and do a terminal value. This assumption needs to be checked by looking at the historical stability of the multiples that are being used for the terminal value calculation. The greater the historical variability of multiples, the greater the error that will be likely in the terminal value. So, one should choose the multiples that have been the most stable, and these usually vary from industry to industry.

6.4 Weighted Average Cost of Capital (WACC)

The APV approach is a very useful tool when we know the debt level that will be used for a project.[8] In this case, the calculation of the tax shield value portion of the APV calculation is feasible and usually straightforward. However, we run into a problem if the capital structure for an asset we are valuing is not known in terms of a level or schedule but rather as a policy.

For example, if we are valuing a firm, we might typically expect the firm to maintain a certain debt ratio through time rather than a certain debt level (or schedule of debt). The application of the APV concept would separate the valuation of the free cash flows and the valuation of the tax shield. The valuation of the tax shield assumes a debt schedule of some kind so that one knows how much debt is expected to be on the balance sheet in the future. With this future level of debt and the associated cost of debt, an interest tax shield can be computed each year. However, with a fixed debt ratio policy, the amount of debt in the future is unknown. This is because the debt level in the future is tied to the asset value in the future (because the debt level is proportional to the asset value when a fixed debt ratio policy is followed). Of course, the asset value in the future is unknown. We do not know the value of the asset today (hence the reason we are doing a valuation), so certainly we will not know the value of the asset any point in the future either. Thus, if the asset value in the future is not known, we will not know the debt level in the future either; therefore, we will not be able to calculate the tax shield value with the traditional APV approach.

We solve this problem by incorporating the tax shield value calculation directly into the free cash flow valuation step. We do this by integrating the tax shield value directly into the discount rate used to value the free cash flows. This modified discount rate is called the weighted average cost of capital, or WACC. With the use of WACC, the APV approach can be implemented in one calculation rather than the two separate calculations that is normally required. However, it is important to note that the use of WACC is only appropriate when the asset to be valued has a capital structure policy where a fixed debt ratio will be used. In all other situations, the traditional APV approach must be utilized.

We will derive the WACC approach[9] through the following simple scenario. Consider the APV approach in the case of a project lasting a single year. The value of this project is given by

$$APV = \frac{FCF}{1+R_A} + \frac{\tau R_D D}{1+R} \tag{16}$$

This equation states the usual APV approach. The second term in this equation is the tax shield value, which comes from the $D of debt on the right side of the balance sheet of this project. The tax rate is given by τ. Notice that the discount rate associated with the tax shield is not R_D. This is because we have not specified a capital structure policy yet. Once we specify the capital structure policy, we will be able to determine this discount rate.

Suppose that the financial policy that is implemented for this project is one that keeps its debt ratio fixed at a constant level d permanently. In this case, $\frac{D}{A} = d$, where A is the usual asset value. Rearranging this expression, we have that

$$D = dA \tag{17}$$

We can now substitute for D into the earlier APV equation:

$$APV = \frac{FCF}{1 + R_A} + \frac{\tau R_D dA}{1 + R} \tag{18}$$

With the capital structure policy known, we can now figure out what the discount rate for the tax shield should be. The tax shield cash flow is given by $\tau R_D dA$. Assuming that the tax rate, the cost of debt capital, and the capital structure policy are fixed, the only quantity that can vary (and thereby create risk) is A. Therefore, the discount rate that appropriately reflects this risk is R_A. So, the full APV formula is given by

$$APV = \frac{FCF}{1 + R_A} + \frac{\tau R_D dA}{1 + R_A} \tag{19}$$

Because APV is simply the value of the left side of the balance sheet, we can simply replace APV with asset value, or A:

$$A = \frac{FCF}{1 + R_A} + \frac{\tau R_D dA}{1 + R_A} \tag{20}$$

We will now solve this equation for A:

$$A = \frac{FCF}{1 + R_A - \tau R_D d} \tag{21}$$

We will eliminate R_A in this equation by using the asset cost of capital formula derived in the previous chapter

$$R_A = \frac{D}{A} R_D + \frac{E}{A} R_E \tag{22}$$

where E denotes equity value. Substituting for R_A in Equation 21 yields

$$A = \frac{FCF}{1 + \frac{D}{A}R_D + \frac{E}{A}R_E - \tau R_D d} \tag{23}$$

We can replace the term d with $\frac{D}{A}$:

$$A = \frac{FCF}{1 + \frac{D}{A}R_D + \frac{E}{A}R_E - \tau R_D \frac{D}{A}}, \tag{24}$$

Rearranging the denominator then gives us a final formula for calculating A, or the APV:

$$A = \frac{FCF}{1 + \frac{D}{A}(1 - \tau)R_D + \frac{E}{A}R_E} \tag{25}$$

Notice that the expression $\frac{D}{A}(1 - \tau)R_D + \frac{E}{A}R_E$ is very similar to the formula for the asset cost of capital. However, it has an extra $(1 - \tau)$ in it multiplying the cost of debt. This expression is commonly known as the *weighted average cost of capital*, or WACC.

$$R_{WACC} = \frac{D}{A}(1 - \tau)R_D + \frac{E}{A}R_E \tag{26}$$

What differentiates WACC from R_A is that WACC includes the tax shield into the discount rate by reducing the cost of debt. We can now rewrite Equation 25 as simply

$$A = \frac{FCF}{1 + R_{WACC}} \tag{27}$$

The use of WACC has effectively eliminated the two-step calculation process typically used in APV and replaced it with a one-step process where the discount rate on the free cash flows is WACC rather than R_A. Therefore, the WACC-based approach is simpler to implement and at the same time eliminates the difficulty discussed earlier of calculating APV in a situation where the debt ratio is held constant.

For simplicity, we have done this calculation for a one-year project (with only one free cash flow and one tax shield cash flow). However, it is easy to show that this derivation can also be done for multiyear projects as well. Therefore, we have the following general formula for valuing assets when a fixed debt ratio policy is in place:

$$APV = \frac{FCF_1}{1+R_{W\,ACC}} + \frac{FCF_2}{(1+R_{W\,ACC})^2} + \frac{FCF_3}{(1+R_{W\,ACC})^3} + \ldots$$

$$(28)$$

Again, keep in mind that the WACC-based approach is simply a special case of the general APV approach. It can only be used in situations where one wants to calculate an APV and the asset being valued has a capital structure policy where a constant debt *ratio* is maintained.

We now demonstrate the WACC-based valuation approach by valuing ABC Co. again. This is done in Figure 6.6.

Figure 6.6 WACC Valuation of ABC Co.

Financial Projections ($MM)

	2013	2014	2015	2016	2017	2018
Net Revenue		11,664	12,831	14,114	15,525	17,077
COGS		8,940	9,834	10,818	11,899	13,089
R&D		298	328	361	397	437
SG&A		1,234	1,358	1,494	1,643	1,807
Other Expenses		304	335	368	405	445
EBIT		887	976	1,073	1,181	1,299
Taxes		188	207	228	251	276
EBIAT		699	768	845	930	
NWC		53	58	64	71	78
Change in NWC		5	5	6	6	7

Financial Projections ($MM)

	2013	2014	2015	2016	2017	2018
PP&E (BoY)		8,895	9,785	10,274	10,788	11,327
Capital Expenditures		1,383	1,032	1,084	1,138	1,195
Depreciation		494	543	570	599	629
PP&E (EoY)		9,785	10,274	10,788	11,327	11,893
FCF		−196	274	326	384	−573
TV (g = 4%)						−13,252
WACC = 8.5%						
PV(FCF + TV)		−180	233	255	277	−9,195
Enterprise Value	**−8,610**					
Debt Value	**3,339**					
Equity Value	**− 11,949**					

Figure 6.6 contains the same free cash flows as Figure 6.3, where we valued ABC Co. using APV with a growing perpetuity terminal value. However, we now assume a more realistic debt policy. In Figure 6.3, we assumed that the debt level was fixed at $4,812M from 2018 onward. Now in Figure 6.6, we assume that ABC Co. always maintains a fixed debt ratio. So, we can simply use WACC to calculate ABC's enterprise value. A WACC of 8.5% is assumed for ABC. The terminal value of free cash flows is calculated using the growing perpetuity formula where we use WACC in place of R_A:

$$TV_{WACC} = \frac{FCF_n(1+g)}{WACC - g} \tag{29}$$

We assume the same growth rate as used in Figure 6.3: 4%. Thus, we arrive at a terminal value of $10,387M. We then calculate the present value of each of the free cash flows and terminal value by discounting at the WACC. The sum of these present values is ABC's enterprise value, $7,791M. No separate calculation for determining tax shield value needs to be done because it is already incorporated in the WACC. ABC's resulting equity value is $4,452M.

6.5 Flow to Equity

The flow to equity (FTE) approach to valuation is widely used in certain financial circles, such as in the context of private equity transactions. FTE is another approach to dealing with the tax shield calculation. With traditional APV, the tax shield is a separate calculation that is added to the free cash flow valuation to arrive at the total asset value. In the case where there is a fixed debt ratio for capital structure policy, the calculation of the tax shield value can be internalized into the discount rate used for free cash flow valuation. This is the WACC approach, and it allows for the application of APV in one calculation rather than two separate ones. The FTE approach is similar to the WACC approach in that it allows for application of the APV approach in one step rather than two separate steps. However with the FTE approach, the tax shield value calculation is internalized into the free cash flows rather than the discount rate.

When we are valuing a company or a project, we are usually really after the value of the equity component of the project. With APV and WACC, we determine this equity value by first determining the value of the asset (because free cash flows are cash flows flowing from the asset to both debt and equity) and then subtracting out the debt value that is used to finance the company or project. FTE instead determines the value of equity directly by looking at just the cash flow to equity (rather than to both equity and debt). Therefore, all cash flows to debt holders are netted out of free cash flows each year to determine the cash flow to equity holders. Figure 6.7 provides a depiction of the cash flow to equity. Because the cash flows to debt are subtracted out, the resulting cash flows are quite different from free cash flows.

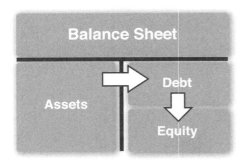

Figure 6.7 Balance sheet view of flow to equity

To determine the cash flow to equity holders, we need to modify the free cash flow formula we have developed. The free cash flow formula is

$$FCF = EBIAT + Depr - \Delta NWC - CapEx \qquad (30)$$

To get to cash flows to equity holders, we need to subtract out all flows to debt holders. There are two types of flows to debt holders: interest and principal. We will subtract out interest by modifying EBIAT to reflect earnings with interest taken out. This would be earnings after taxes, or simply net income. Therefore, instead of EBIAT, we would use net income. The second change to the free cash flow formula is to net out any principal payments. Principal payments on debt decrease the cash available for distribution to equity holders. This is why principal payments need to be subtracted out to arrive at the cash flow to equity holders. These two changes would result in the following cash flow formula:

$$FTE = NI + Depr - \Delta NWC - CapEx + \Delta Debt \qquad (31)$$

NI denotes net income, and $\Delta Debt$ denotes the increase in debt level.[10]

The final question we need to answer is what is the appropriate discount rate. The value of equity is determined entirely by cash flows to equity because these are the only cash flows equity holders receive. In fact, using the present value relation, Equation 1, we can write down the value of equity today (time 0) as the discounted value of cash flows to equity:

$$Equity_0 = \frac{E(FTE_1)}{1+r} + \frac{E(FTE_2)}{(1+r)^2} + \frac{(FTE_3)}{(1+r)^3} + \ldots$$

(32)

Therefore, the riskiness of equity comes entirely from the riskiness of FTE. So, the riskiness of FTE must be equal to the riskiness of equity. If this is the case, then the appropriate cost of capital to discount FTE must be the equity cost of capital. So, we have

$$Equity_0 = \frac{E(FTE_1)}{1+R_E} + \frac{E(FTE_2)}{(1+R_E)^2} + \frac{(FTE_3)}{(1+R_E)^3} + \ldots$$

(33)

When we apply the FTE approach, we do not need to calculate a separate tax shield cash flow because the tax shield is already embedded in net income (NI). The only complication we need to worry about is a terminal value calculation, but we can do this using a growing perpetuity approach. We demonstrate the FTE approach in Figure 6.8 by valuing ABC Co. again, but utilizing the FTE approach.

Figure 6.8 Flow to Equity Valuation of ABC Co.'s Equity

Financial Projections ($MM)						
	2013	2014	2015	2016	2017	2018
Net Revenue		11,664	12,831	14,114	15,525	17,077
COGS		8,940	9,834	10,818	11,899	13,089
R&D		298	328	361	397	437
SG&A		1,234	1,358	1,494	1,643	1,807
Other Expenses		304	335	368	405	445
EBIT		887	976	1,073	1,181	1,299
Interest Expense		215	231	249	268	289
Taxes		143	158	175	194	
Net Income		529	587	650	719	1,010

Financial Projections ($MM)

	2013	2014	2015	2016	2017	2018
NWC		53	58	64	71	78
Change in NWC		5	5	6	6	7
PP&E (BoY)		8,895	9,785	10,274	10,788	11,327
Capital Expenditures		1,383	1,032	1,084	1,138	1,195
Depreciation		494	543	570	599	629
PP&E (EoY)		9,785	10,274	10,788	11,327	11,893
CCF		–365	92	130	173	437
Flow to Equity		–120	359	422	493	786
TV						8,170
R(E) = 14%						
PV(FCF + TV)		–108	291	309	325	5,315
Debt Level		3,584	3,851	4,143	4,463	4,812
R(D) = 6%						
Interest Payment		215	231	249	268	289

Equity Value   **6,132**

Notice that in the upper part of this figure, we have net income now instead of EBIAT. To calculate net income, we have subtracted out the interest payment on debt. In the lower part of Figure 6.8, we have the debt level for each year (which comes from the projections in Figure 3.1.1). We calculate the interest expense by assuming a cost of debt capital of 6% and multiplying this by the debt level. For example in 2014, the interest expense is $3,584 \times 6\% = 215$. From the NI value, we subtract out the changes in net working capital and capital expenditures, and add back depreciation to arrive at a number sometimes referred to as *capital cash flows* (CCF). From CCF, we subtract out the change in debt level for that year to arrive at the flow to equity.[11] We now need to calculate a terminal value in 2018. We do this using the growing perpetuity formula for FTE:

$$TV_{FTE} = \frac{FTE_n(1+g)}{R_E - g}$$

$$(34)$$

The cost of equity is assumed to be 14%, and we use the standard growth rate of 4%. This gives a terminal value of \$5,939M. We now present value each of the equity cash flows and the terminal value at the cost of equity. Summing these present values then produces the value of ABC Co.'s equity, \$4,680M. As discussed earlier, there was no need to do a separate tax shield cash flow because it was already captured in the net income.

Endnotes

1. The total asset value is equal to the operating asset value plus the value of the tax shield.

$$A = OA + TS$$

However, recall from the previous chapter that our working assumption is that the tax shield value is substantially smaller than the value of the operating assets. In this case the total asset value, A, is approximately equal to the operating asset value, OA:

$$A = OA + TS$$

$$\approx OA$$

We can follow a similar logic with the cost of assets:

$$R_A = \frac{OA}{OA+TS}R_O A + \frac{TS}{OA+TS}R_T S$$

$$\approx R_{OA}$$

If the tax shield value is small relative to the value of operating assets, the operating asset cost of capital is approximately equal to the asset cost of capital.

2. There is no rule as to what point in time this truncation should occur. One rule that is used when changing or restructuring an asset is to work out the detailed cash flows until the changes have all been fully implemented. Another common rule is to truncate when one loses visibility on (or loses sufficient confidence in the accuracy of) forecasted future financial statements.

3. It is important to note that the cost of capital for the project is not the same as the cost of capital for ABC Co. If the project has a risk profile that differs from ABC, the cost of capital has to be calculated using comparables similar to the project rather than to ABC.

4. Otherwise, the rate of free cash flow growth is so high that it causes the terminal value to have infinite value.

5. Enterprise value is another way of referring to the asset value of the firm.

6. We assume that this calculation was done using the techniques described in Chapter 5, "Cost of Capital."

7. EBITDA refers to *earnings before interest, taxes, depreciation, and amortization.* EBITDA is similar to EBIT, but it tries to strip out all noncash expenses as well. Therefore, EBITDA is sometimes used as a measure of operating cash flow.

8. Note that the debt level may be fixed or there could be a debt schedule (where the debt level either increases or decreases in a predetermined manner).

9. Although we treat this approach as one that is distinct from APV, note that this is not really the case. The WACC approach is really a subset of the APV approach. It is a quick (one-step) way to implement APV when the capital structure policy is stipulated to maintain a fixed debt ratio. Therefore, it is more correct to refer to the WACC approach as a WACC-based APV approach.

10. Principal repayments would result in a negative value for $\Delta Debt$, so the application of this formula would result in principal repayments decreasing cash flows to equity, as we expect.

11. In Figure 6.8, the 2013 debt level is $3,339M, which comes from Figure 3.1.1.

Index

FINANCIAL TIMES

In an increasingly competitive world, it is quality of thinking that gives an edge—an idea that opens new doors, a technique that solves a problem, or an insight that simply helps make sense of it all.

We work with leading authors in the various arenas of business and finance to bring cutting-edge thinking and best-learning practices to a global market.

It is our goal to create world-class print publications and electronic products that give readers knowledge and understanding that can then be applied, whether studying or at work.

To find out more about our business products, you can visit us at www.ftpress.com.